DAD ACADEMY

RAISING COURAGEOUS CAPABLE CONFIDENT KIDS

JEFF HAMILTON

© 2025

Dedicated to...

POP (Jack)

for showing me what a dad is

and along with Mom,

guiding me to discover

who God has made me to be

JAYME

for marrying me

and giving my life meaning

BEAR (Justin) **& SIS** (Jordanne)

for making me a dad

and giving my life a

greater purpose

TABLE OF
Contents

Meet MEA   *006*

WHY DAD ACADEMY?   *008*
Introduction

Meet NICK   *012*

01 **LEAVING A LEGACY**   *014*
Starting with The End in Mind

Meet BRAD   *036*

02 **PARENTING PARTNERSHIP**   *038*
Honoring Your Parenting Partner

Meet SEAN   *062*

03 DESTINY DECISIONS 064

Choosing Your Parenting Path

Meet FRITZ 084

04 DEVELOPING CHARACTER 086

Building Trust and Cultivating Courage

Meet CORY 108

05 CREATING COMPETENCY 110

Preparing Kids for Life

Meet TIM 134

06 INSTILLING CONFIDENCE 136

Producing a Healthy Family Culture

Meet CHRIS 158

07 MAKING LIFE MEMORABLE 160

Milestone Moments and Significant Ceremonies

Meet GORDY 182

08 The DAD PLAN™ 184

Meet DARREN 214

AKNOWLEGEMENTS 216

One of the biggest lessons I learned through Dad Academy is that I don't need to have all the answers—I just need to be purposeful about my parenting.

I became a father at 24, living in a low-income apartment and relying on public assistance. Fatherhood doesn't come with a manual, and I quickly realized how unprepared I felt. My wife and I were just barely making ends meet, covering our bills month to month. On top of that, I was still processing my own childhood trauma. I **had to figure out how to break the cycle and ensure that my past didn't negatively impact how I raised my own children.**

I grew up in a big family. If we went somewhere, we went as a family. It felt like we were always on the move—either in a basketball gym or on a baseball field. Unfortunately, that sense of togetherness ended when I was in seventh grade. My dad was an alcoholic, and his struggles led to verbal and physical abuse toward my mom. When she entered a new relationship, my father spiraled even further into addiction, and our family fractured. I ended up living with friends and family members who, thankfully, became strong male role models in my life. Some of these men I still call "Dad" today. They taught me core values like loyalty, hard work, and discipline—lessons that have shaped the man and father I am today.

One of the biggest lessons I learned through Dad Academy is that I don't need to have all the answers—I just need to be purposeful about my parenting. I've always planned for work, for coaching, for just about everything else in life. But I never thought about planning as a dad. **Sitting down with my spouse and creating a parenting plan changed everything for us.** It gave us clarity, direction, and a shared vision for how we wanted to raise our kids. As the father of two boys and a girl, I'm focused on what I can do to support the dreams of my children, how I can challenge them, push them, motivate them, and love them through it all.

Dad Academy reinforces how important it is to be intentional in all aspects of fatherhood. One of my favorite traditions that has come out of this journey is our morning prayer time. Every day on the way to school, we pray together as a family. We take turns, but we never force anyone to pray. Sometimes, my children will volunteer, even my five-year-old, and I love hearing his little prayers. In fact, on the busiest mornings, it's often him who reminds us to pray. That is legacy.

Dad Academy hasn't just strengthened my relationship with my children; it has also given me a new perspective. Perhaps the most unexpected blessing is that it has helped me restore my once-broken relationship with my own father. I can now proudly say that, at the time of this writing, he is 10 years sober. And for that, I am incredibly grateful.

WHY DAD ACADEMY

On March 1, 1996, I entered a new season of life as I held my newborn baby boy. My wife Jayme and I had taken some parenting classes to help prepare us for the first few months with a newborn. **But as I felt the weight of holding my son in my arms, my soul felt another weight - that of immense responsibility.** I remember feeling overwhelming love and joy, followed by a serious concern about my ability to be a dad. Those same feelings appeared again on May 5, 1998 when my daughter was placed in my arms.

In the fall of 1999, my wife and I relocated across the country for work. I needed to find a way to supplement my income until the startup I was founding got off the ground. I also wanted to find a way to build relationships in our new community. So, I found a flexible job with a well-known coffee shop chain. But my first day on the job wasn't at the store. Instead, it was in a classroom where I spent the next week learning about coffee and the culture of the company.

Let me connect some dots in the story...I was required to undergo forty hours of training before I was qualified to push the "brew" button on the automated coffee maker in the store, but the doctor just handed me my babies and wished me good luck? There had to be a better way.

I had an advantage over most men. My wife and I were both raised with loving dads who were great examples of what a father should be. And while neither of them would say they were perfect, **their consistent presence in our lives gave us confidence in our identity and abilities.**

The first decade of my career was spent working with adolescents and their families. I saw the struggles that many families experienced first-hand as they navigated the challenges of the pre-teen and teenage years. **I witnessed the impact that unhealthy marriages have on children and the effect of dads not being present in the home.** I also saw families that were winning at home. Much of that had to do with a father's presence and engagement in the lives of his children.

I had a mental catalogue of things to do and not to do as a dad through the various seasons of life that my kids experienced. While I did my best, I was far from perfect. What I did try to be as a father was to be an intentional one. And I watched my children grow into independent, confident young adults. After they graduated from high school, I thought that there were some things to offer to men who may not have had the advantages I did, or who wanted to be more purposeful in their parenting.

A man once said, *"Being a father is the most important thing I will ever do and if I don't do this well, no other thing I do really matters."* It's proven that in the lives of children and in communities that #dadmatters. You, Dad, matter. So let's get to work in changing our families….for good.

○ dad.academy   𝕏 dadacademy

f dadacademy   ▶ dadacademyonline

♪ dadacademy   ⊕ **dadacademy.info**

One of the most powerful lessons I've learned is that my presence as a father matters more than I ever realized.

I can still remember the moment I realized my definition of family was shaped more by separation than togetherness. Both of my parents came from divorced homes, and their own marriage followed the same heartbreaking pattern. For what felt like at least a year, my parents were split, and I lived with my mom, siblings, and grandparents—my mom's mom and stepdad. Stability felt fragile, as if the smallest disruption could send everything crumbling. When outside influences upset my parents, our world would shrink. Isolation became normal. I learned early on that love sometimes felt conditional and that conflict often led to withdrawal rather than resolution.

As a father, I strive not to repeat my parents' mistakes, yet I often find myself slipping into familiar patterns. When life feels overwhelming, my instinct is to withdraw, much like my parents did. I've caught myself trying to control my family's environment rather than nurturing them through challenges. Fear of failure sometimes drives me to overcorrect, creating distance rather than connection. I want to provide my children with security and peace, but I've realized that my desire for control can sometimes create an emotional gap between us. The hardest part has been recognizing that love isn't just about protection—it's about presence, even in the messiness of life.

Through Dad Academy, I've learned that fatherhood isn't about perfection—it's about partnership. I must truly partner with my wife, working together rather than in isolation. More importantly, I've realized that I can't lead my family well if I'm relying solely on my own strength. I must be led by the Holy Spirit, allowing God to guide me as I seek to create a home filled with wholeness and peace. Rather than withdrawing when challenges arise, I'm learning to lean in, to communicate openly, and to love unconditionally.

One of the most powerful lessons I've learned is that my **presence** as a father matters more than I ever realized. It's in the small moments—the bedtime stories, the prayers before school, the shared laughter at the dinner table—that true connection is built. My kids don't need me to have all the answers; they just need me to be there, fully engaged, showing up day after day.

My goal is no longer just to avoid repeating the past but to build something new—a family built on faith, love, and unwavering commitment. I want my children to grow up knowing that home is a place of refuge, where they are seen, heard, and deeply loved. **And for me, that starts with being the father God has called me to be—imperfect but present,** learning as I go, and trusting that with His guidance, I can lead my family well.

CHAPTER

01

Leaving a Legacy

Starting with The End in Mind

"

Every father should
remember that one day
his children will follow
his example instead of
his advice.

CHARLES F. KETTERING

LEAVING A LEGACY

Starting with The End in Mind

---

*T*here are two roles most men will play for the majority of our lives - husbands and dads. Yet, being a dad is the only job we have that comes with absolutely zero training. Everything we learn is on the job. Men are most successful when the terms are defined, the expectations are clarified, and the goal is in sight. The Dad Academy process is designed to help you find success as a father, or grandfather, and to help you be a better man to everyone in your circle of influence.

DAD IS DESTINY

There's a saying that "dad is destiny," and without diminishing the significant role of mothers, research proves this out. *Research from the University of Pennsylvania indicates that children who feel closeness and warmth with their father are twice as likely to enter college, 75% less likely to have a child in their teen years, 80% less likely to be incarcerated, and half as likely to show signs of depression.*[1] Other studies find an active nurturing and style of fathering is associated with better verbal skills in children, intellectual functioning, and

---

[1] Booth, A., Scott, M. E., & King, V. (2010). "Father Residence and Adolescent Problem Behavior: Are Youth Always Better Off in Two-Parent Families?" Journal of family issues, 31(5), 585-605.

academic achievement among adolescents. *In an analysis of over 100 studies on parent child relationships, researchers found that having a loving and nurturing father was as important for a child's happiness, well-being, social, and academic success as having a loving and nurturing mother.*[2] Some studies even show that a father's love was a stronger contributor to important positive child well-being outcomes. If these findings are true, and the research proves they are, then men need to learn how to be the best dad they can be. Unfortunately, there's not a lot of practical training on how to be a dad.

When my children were in pre-school, I was hired for a part-time job at Starbucks. At that time the onboarding training process took thirty hours to be qualified to pour coffee for somebody (see the Preface). What if fathers were required to invest that kind of time, not only in an orientation class, but also had a tool to help them strategize going forward as their children grew that gave dads confidence that they were informed and equipped to be the best that they could be? That would be an investment that will benefit men and their families for the rest of their lives.

PROMISES OF DAD ACADEMY

I want to make four promises to you about Dad Academy.

1. When you've finished this book, you'll understand your mission as a dad.

2. You'll know how to prepare your kids for adulthood.

---

[2] Ronald P. Rohner and A. Veneziano, "The Importance of Father Love: History and Contemporary Evidence," Review of General Psychology 5.4 (2001): 382-405.

3. You'll be able to define your family culture and create memories that will last a lifetime.

4. If you complete the guidebook section at the end of each chapter you will develop your own personal dad plan and a year's worth of intentional memory making moments.

WHAT IS YOUR GOAL FOR YOUR FAMILY?

So the "how" begins with having what our end goal is in sight. What are we shooting for? The question I want to ask you today is: what do you want for your kids? What are your hopes and dreams for your family and your children? Other generations before us simply expressed that they wanted their children to do better than they did. With that in mind, **what does "do better" mean for you?**

Your Turn

_____

_____

_____

I do know that every dad simply wants their kids to be happy and to be successful, and in order for those things to happen, someone is going to have to show them how to get there, and that's you, Dad.

In fact, that's the whole job of being a dad. Fatherhood is about the leadership you provide to your family. It's not just about management. It's more than just doing the things right. It's learning how to do the right things. When it comes to our kids and our families, the right things are not just about setting goals or accomplishing things. It's really understanding and determining what's important: identifying the life skills you'll pass on to your children and the values that you're going to live by.

DEFINING YOUR MISSION AS A DAD

The Bible offers helpful direction for fathers. In the ancient wisdom book called Proverbs, the writer says, *"Train up a child in the way that he should go, and when he is old, he'll not depart from it."* Another version says it this way, *"Teach children in a way that fits their needs, and even when they're old, they will not leave the right path."*[3] Dads, this reminds us of our purpose, that we have a responsibility to train our children. This means helping them learn how to live life with courage, to develop skills that will make them feel competent as they navigate through life, and to cultivate a clear sense of self and confidence. This training happens not only by creating intentional learning opportunities, but also by being available and accessible in the everyday rhythms of life. They may pick up what we know, but they will become what we are.

Have you had people tell you that your children resemble you? That was a common comment I received from people even into my adult years. It's not

---

[3] Proverbs 22:6 (Easy-To-Read Version).

that I looked like my dad, but many of my mannerisms, from the way I talk to literally the way I walk (this kind of ex-athlete stroll), resembled his. I tend to process decisions like my father. All this is from the imprint he made on my life.

There's a saying that says "more is caught than taught", and this is especially true from a child's perspective. They learn what is important by watching us, observing what we do, and how we respond to situations and to relationships. Eventually they're going to embrace those values, because they're going to repeat what they see. Children are trained in what is important by what they see repeated over and over. These are the values of their family.

The training of our children also needs to be individualized to meet their needs. Dads can't just be one size fits all. This means that dad's not just about being fair, being equal, but it is about him being just. **You know, the statistics tell us that the most important thing you can do with your life is to be the best dad that you can be, and that is your life's mission.** If the Bible is our guidebook, then we also have a model in Jesus.

Jesus had a mission statement: *"For the Son of Man did not come to be served, but to serve and to give his life as a ransom for many."*[4] What was important to Jesus? What did Jesus train his followers to do when a choice had to be made? What guided his choices? Here, Jesus defined his life's purpose as serving, as giving his life away. He modeled this belief by his behavior.

---

[4] Mark 10:44-45; Matthew 20:28 (NIV)

Fatherhood is leadership, not management. It not only doing things right, but doing the right things.

Jesus lived out his values. Because he believed that serving was important, he gave his disciples a practical example of service. They came to dinner one night. Jesus put a towel around his waist, took the bowl of water that was near the door, and bent down, (as was the custom in that tradition), and washed the disciples' feet. *Now, this task was usually performed by a servant in the house, but in this case, Jesus became the servant.*[5] Then he told them, through his example and his words, that their greatness was going to be found in serving. I often wonder if every time the disciples put on their shoes, they were reminded about their life's purpose, and how they were going to find greatness and significance because of Jesus's example. **Your mission must be connected to action.** Your values are based in a belief about what is truly important in life. Your values will be transferred by both your words and your actions. Let's be clear - a father's mission is to transfer their values and skills to their kids. So consider these questions:

1. What's important for you to pass on to your kids?
2. How do you communicate it and how do you model it?

DEFINING FAMILY VALUES

The first thing we're going to have to define in our dad plan journey is our values. You might be asking, what are values? For this purpose, values are the belief behind your behavior. They're the why behind the what. A man's values develop over their lifetime, until they become subconsciously integrated into

---

[5] John 13:1-17

every area of our lives. These values are shaped by our life's experience, both positive and negative. They're shaped by the things that inspire us, stimulate us, and motivate us to action. Values may be reflected even in the things that capture our attention, like our interests or hobbies. I describe the feeling associated with these things as being like *"when I do this, I feel the most like me."* That's why when we make a choice to do some things, to think a certain way and to avoid other things and feelings, it's because those choices are based in our values.

"DAD WINS"

While I'd like to think the best of my intentions will be the thing that my family picks up on, the truth is our actual behavior reveals our values and programs our family to respond to them. During the pandemic, my daughter, who had just graduated college, was at home with my wife and me. I was working on some things on my computer and I heard my wife and daughter chatting in the kitchen about what we should have for dinner. I heard my daughter suggest that we add broccoli as a side dish. My wife said, "You know Dad doesn't like broccoli." That's true (for a number of reasons). They continued on with the conversation and I continued on with my work.

The next day there was similar scenario, where the girls were chatting in the other room. I don't remember what they were talking about as my focus was on the sporting event I was watching. I do remember my daughter commenting to my wife, "That's not Dad's kind of thing." Since I didn't know what they were discussing, I let it go without jumping in.

Again, the following day my daughter and wife were talking and I was working in the other room. I can't remember the topic of their conversation, but I remember what my wife said to my daughter - "that's not something your Dad would like." Immediately I heard another voice, an internal one that whispered "Dad wins." I broke, because I knew that was one of the default values of our home. Everyone in my home knew what I liked and didn't like. Rather than my desire to serve my family's needs, our family had built their decisions around my preferences because I had unintentionally set up our culture for there to only be one winner - me. I realized that there needed to be a change, and the change had to start with me. So I've been working to build my life around what was important to the most important people in my life.

Being a dad is making choices based on a set of values that help you to determine what is important and directs our response. We must come to the realization that every decision a man makes is actually two decisions; the decision to do something is also the choice not to do something else. So, it is important to understand how

> **Values are the belief behind your behavior. They're the "why" behind the "what."**

to make choices that reflect our values, that we put into action.

YOUR VALUES ARE BASED IN YOUR CHOICES

There's a leader in the Bible named Joshua. Joshua received the leadership of the people from his mentor Moses, and led the nation into a new destiny and identity. At the end of his life, Joshua said this to the people that he had served for his lifetime: *"If serving the Lord seems undesirable to you, then choose for yourself this day whom you will serve, whether the gods your ancestors served back before you didn't know God or the gods of the culture of the land. But as for me and my house, we will serve the Lord."*[6]

Notice the importance that Joshua gave to the choices that would have to be made by the heads of families, usually the fathers. Every father has to make choices. But a father's choices are important because they have a direct impact on all those who are entrusted to your care. In Dad Academy, you will learn how to make the choices that are necessary to accomplish your mission and prepare your kids for the life that you hope and dream for them.

DISCOVERING YOUR VALUES

Every part of our life, the roles and responsibilities we have, our interests and hobbies, our life goals and measurement for success is integrated by one's values. Values are not what you want (aspirational), they are what you do (actual).

[6] Joshua 24:15 (author paraphrase)

These values serve as the core for our lives. In determining your values, two questions must be answered:

1. **WHAT** is important? and,
2. **WHY** is it important?

The "what" is often the measurement, while the "why" speaks to the motivation. For example, you may consider "hard work" to be a value. The question then needs to be asked: why is it a value? Is it because you work hard to receive recognition or validation? Or is it because hard work is a reflection of one's character, diligence, and dedication? If it's the latter, consider rephrasing the value as "diligence" or "industriousness" or "faithfulness." These words reflect an approach to life more than simply a desired intent.

When your values are defined you'll have a better sense about who you are and what it is of true value that you have that you have to pass on to your kids.

REFLECTION
Questions ★ ★ ★

1 What values do you want to pass on to your children, and why are they important to you?

2 How do your daily actions and decisions currently reflect the values you want to instill in your family?

Think about a moment when your child mirrored your behavior—was it a positive or negative reflection? What did you learn from it?

How can you model leadership in your home, not just by managing tasks, but by shaping the culture and values of your family?

HOME WORK

Identify Your Core Values

Discovering your core values is a vital step toward becoming a more intentional father. Your values serve as guiding principles, shaping your decisions and behaviors. Here's a structured process to help you identify and define your personal values:

Step 1

Understand What Values Are

- Values are the beliefs behind your behavior—they are the **"why behind the what"** you do.
- They have been shaped over a lifetime through experiences, inspirations, and motivations.
- Values are not **aspirations** (what you wish you lived by), but **actual behaviors** (what you consistently do).

Step 2
Reflect on Your Life Experiences

Think about your **positive and negative life experiences**. What lessons have shaped who you are?

_____

_____

_____

Identify moments where you felt the most like **your true self**—activities, hobbies, and roles where you felt most alive.

_____

_____

_____

Consider what **inspires you, stimulates you, and motivates you to action.**

_____

_____

_____

Step 3
Answer Two Essential Questions

WHAT is important to me?

(This is the external measurement—what you see and do.)

_____

_____

_____

WHY is it important?

This is the internal motivation—what drives you.)

> *Example:* If you think "hard work" is a value, ask **why** it matters. Is it for recognition? Or
>
> because it reflects your **diligence and dedication**? If it's the latter, your true value might
>
> be **"Diligence" or "Industriousness."**

_____

_____

_____

_____

Step 4
Create Your Personal Values List

Write down a list of 10-15 words that represent values you live by. Use precise words that describe an approach to life, not just a desired outcome. Group similar values together and narrow the list to 3-6 core values.

Step 5

Define and Personalize Your Values

Write a **clear definition** of each of your top values in your own words. Think of a **real-life example** of how you live out each value.

> *Example:* **Value: Generosity** – "My life is about serving others with the skills and resources that are available to me."

Step 6

Define and Personalize Your Values

Assess how well your daily life reflects these values. Are your choices and priorities in alignment?

 **OR**

Identify any **gaps** between what you say you value and what you actually do.

_____

_____

_____

Are these values consistently demonstrated in the roles and relationships in my life?

 **OR**

I've realized my job is not to teach them to be like me; my job is to help them become more of who they already are.

Growing up in a pastor's house, I remember lessons my dad taught me about fatherhood. But I also see how many lessons and ideas I inferred about fatherhood by being a son to my dad, and as they say, "more is caught than taught." He taught me about facing fears and persevering through challenges, he handed me a faith and encouraged me as I made it my own, and he stressed the importance of family. But I also remember him being gone a lot, once for so long once I couldn't recall his face without looking at his picture in the hallway. I remember that his service to others often took precedence over us. And I remember feeling like I couldn't have the relationship I wanted with him because other people needed him more. This "close but distant" relationship influenced my perception of fatherhood. **I knew I wanted to pass on what I was taught, and I knew I had to be intentional about what would be caught.**

Parenting is the single most heart filling and gut-wrenching thing I've done. Being intentional about what gets "caught" has helped me position my parenting away from authoritarianism and towards relationship building with each of my kids. My path to fatherhood wasn't the traditional one; when my wife and I married I was instantly gifted with two girls and two boys. The girls didn't need a father - their dad is alive and well, and their relationship is solid. All they need from me is to know I'm there for them and to see their mom loved well. The boys' father passed away when they were two and a half years and six months old, and I'm beyond grateful to be their dad. We had one more boy, completing our family. Their personalities are all very different, they absorb information differently, they give and receive love differently, and they experience life in ways unique to them. I've realized my job is not to teach them to be like me; my job is to help them become more of who they already are. **Our family "blends" well because we don't consider it blended**. There are no "steps" or "halfs" in our family. There are only brothers, sisters, and love.

Dad Academy is a toolbox, a seed packet, an instruction manual even, on intentional parenting for dads. It reminds us of what we already know, provides creative new ways of thinking about things, and it inspires with exercises and assignments geared towards dads becoming more and more intentional in their parenting. **Dad Academy is about helping dads help kids become the men and women they were born to be.**

CHAPTER

Parenting Partnership

Honoring Your Parenting Partner

"

Live in such a way that
if your children are ever
asked for the definitions
of kindness, integrity, and
loyalty, they'll answer,
"my parents."

ALI B MOE

PARENTING PARTNERSHIP

Honoring Your Parenting Partner

*B*eing an intentional father is like building a house. It takes planning, preparation, hard work, and some help from others. You are building a structure your kids will be able to build their lives on. It all begins with the foundation. For dads, that foundation is understanding the values you have built your life around so that you can intentionally pass them on to your children. What you pass on to your kids is whatever is at the center of your life, not your roles or your responsibilities, but your personal values. And what we don't often understand is that values are not what we want to be, but they actually reflect who you are and what you do.

WHAT'S AT YOUR CORE?

If you are a Christ-follower, you may think that God is at the center of your life. But God is not the special surprise that's hidden inside the Tootsie Pop. It's not where if you dig deep enough, He'll eventually be found like oil under a well. No, in fact, the Scripture says that Christ is all and he's in all.[7] So, Jesus is

---

[7] Colossians 3:11

41

not just at the center of your life. He's integrated into everything in your life. If you're a Christ-follower, he's already in everything that you're doing.

Part of the process of unpacking your values is to discover what God has placed at the core of who you are . **What are those things that make you, you?**

Values have a profound effect on those around you, because what's at your center shapes and drives your behavior and defines your life's mission. To recap, your mission as a father is to intentionally pass on the values and skills you have to them. Preparing them for life is your purpose as a dad.

THE IMPORTANCE OF DAD

Research reminds us of how important dads are to kids. When a dad has a healthy relationship with his daughter, they are less likely to be sexually active.[8] When fathers have a healthy relationship with their sons, these young men are less aggressive, less defiant, and more socially mature. In fact, studies show that in most families, it's also the father who contributes the most to children

[8] Regnerus, Mark D. and Laura B. Luchies. 2006. "The Parent-Child Relationship and Opportunities for Adolescents' First Sex." Journal of Family Issues 27: 159-183.

becoming self-reliant, self-disciplined, and self-motivated.

Brett Copeland, a clinical psychologist in Tacoma, Washington, writes that fathers encourage competition, the ability to take risks, and what we call having courage. **Dads encourage independence and achievement in the lives of their children.** This is not to discount mothers: they encourage equity, sense of security or comfort in a family, and collaboration, the idea of working together.

Both parents' developmental contributions are required to build strong kids. Yet what we discover is Dad's unique assignment. Dads build self confidence in children through encouragement, like pouring courage into them – "You got this! You can do it!". Along with encouragement, Dads provide affirmation. Every child inherently wants to make their father proud,

> Your mission as a father is to intentionally pass on the values and skills you have to them. Preparing them for life is your purpose as a dad.

and it's our responsibility and privilege to let them know they have. Lastly, fathers provide a child's framework for evaluation: Was I successful? What was done well? What are ways to grow? Dads who provide love-based feedback build a child's sense of worth.

THE THREE C's OF PARENTING

Dad, you are responsible for your child's sense of self confidence. They get their sense of value and worth from you. That means that you are responsible to help your children develop these three qualities: courage, competence and confidence. These are the three Cs of what a dad is going to pass on to his children. Moms complement that self-confidence by building awareness of others. Mothers do this through another three Cs they are uniquely equipped to build into the life of their children, compassion, comfort and cooperation. Together, both parents help anchor a child's sense of worth and of value.

> As a father, you are responsible to cultivate courage, competence, and confidence in your children.

Obviously, the roles of father and mother are complementary and necessary for a child's well-being. Unfortunately, without a dad, the other awareness that moms cultivate becomes a self-centeredness, because the child becomes then the center of that world. With an overbearing or completely disengaged dad, self-confidence becomes self-consciousness, because you're always aware that you're being evaluated because you're looking for affirmation from the one who is the model and the example in your life.

DAD AS LIFE-GIVER

To illustrate the interdependent roles of a father and mother, one only needs to consider the roles of male and female in the way that life is conceived. Dad is the seed: the life-giver. Mom is the host: the life-nurturer. I want you to pause to think about this important question - **"What are you bringing or giving life to in your children's lives?"**

_____

_____

_____

Your Turn

Whatever you as a dad direct your energy and effort towards will produce life.

Just as in conception, there are three elements to fertilizing the potential within your children. The first is **quantity**. Think about this, it takes millions of sperm to fertilize one egg, while you only need one to do its job, you don't know which one will take. As a father there are millions of minutes to spend with your child in their lifetime. Some people will say, it's not it's not quantity, it's quality. But really, isn't it both? You need to be able to offer your best as often as you can, with the belief that some of it is going to produce good results.

Whatever you as a dad direct your energy and effort towards will produce life.

Not only is there quantity in the process of giving life, but there's also *timing*.

There are moments that are more important than others. There are times when the egg of life is receptive to what you have to deposit and bring to it. And as a dad, I'm not always able to identify which moment is the right time. For example, having a conversation critiquing your child's athletic performance in the car ride home following a game isn't very productive in most cases. But when your child casually initiates a conversation with a question, that might indicate an opportunity to go deeper. The only way to make the most of those opportunities is to be present for them as the moments arise. A Brigham Young University study says although participation in family leisure activities is important and needed, it was a father's involvement in the everyday home based, common family leisure activities that held more weight than the large, extravagant out of the ordinary types of activities. [9]

When examining how families function and what produces health, it's not only about the big moments, but it only makes a difference when it's combined with the everyday, ordinary interactions that really complements and brings life to your kids. **It is so important for you to look for teachable moments when your kids, their ears and eyes, most importantly, their hearts, are open.** When children are small, you get to create and define those moments. With your teens, you have to respond to the moments as they appear, because

---

[9] CBuswell, L., Zabriskie, R.B., Lundberg, N., & Hawkins, A.J. (2012). "The Relationship Between Father Involvement in Family Leisure and Family Functioning: The Importance of Daily Family Leisure." Leisure Sciences, 34, 172-190.

it's usually on their schedule, not ours. I've found that going for a walk or hike with my daughter created opportunities for us to connect. When her feet were moving, the conversation was flowing. Similarly, activity was the key to heart-to-heart conversation with my son. The goal is to find times when their hearts are open and responsive to the opportunities as they present themselves.

Now, we've spoken about quantity. We've talked about timing. The last element is **persistence**. You just keep loving them until eventually you break through that hard shell and are able to fertilize the life that's in them. A seed's life is never done. In fact, Jesus says it this way, "unless a seed falls to the ground and dies, it never can produce life". It is crucial for us to understand those three life-giving principles.

It's not only important to understand the roles of dad and mom, but also to consider the relational dynamic between dad and mom. If you're going to be a good father, you're going to want to know how to best partner with your child's mother as you raise your kids. To be a good partner requires us to step into and understand mom's world a little bit.

REAL LIFE OUTSIDE OF PARADISE

To do so, let's start with a discussion about the very first mom, Eve. According to the Bible, after Adam and Eve have sinned and been expelled from the Garden, we get our first look at what life is like outside of paradise. The author of Genesis captures the moment like this: *"Now Adam knew Eve, his wife, and she conceived and bore Cain and said, "I have acquired a man from the Lord.""*.[10] This is the first description of marital intimacy in the scripture, and the result of this kind of intimacy is procreation. Life is given. Yet Eve's response is that God and I have done something special. Maybe she sees this as an opportunity to reform the mistakes that she sees in Adam. We read from the sacred text that God makes humankind in His own image. Could it be that without a sense of relational integrity, women form children into their own image? Women have a different set of values, a different set of priorities, and when those needs are not met in their lives, they want to make sure that they are met in the lives of their kids.

When God gave Eve to Adam, they were helpmates; they were equal partners. God's direction to them was to be fruitful and multiply, to subdue the earth, to fill it, and to have dominion over it. When Adam and Eve take things into their own hands and violate the relationship, God confronts them. In that moment Adam could have taken responsibility, but didn't. Instead, he blamed the woman; it was Eve's fault. Adam deflected accountability not only for his own actions but his responsibility to the relationship with Eve (and God) when he replied to God's question with *"She gave it to me."*[11] What do you think resulted from Adam's response? Did it build trust? Did it build security? Did it build confidence? Or did it damage the partnership that God intended between Adam and Eve?

---

[10] Genesis 4:1 (NKJV)
[11] Genesis 3:8-13

I want to tell you that **you can redeem your family by taking responsibility for it and by being a helpmate to your children's mother,** whether you're married to her or not. No more excuses, no more blame, no more running from responsibility. The reason why understanding what's at the center of our life is so important is because those things influence your relationship with your kids and shape the relationship with their mother.

THE CO-PARENTING CHALLENGE

Maybe you find yourself in one of those difficult situations where you are co-parenting with another parent, where your kids are not under the same roof as a family. Maybe you're trying to be a dad and co-parent with your spouse to her own children from a previous relationship. Both scenarios are challenging. And they are complicated by the trauma of divorce.

Most people don't consider the impact that divorce has on dads. *Many people are surprised to learn men are more likely than women to become depressed, to develop a stress related illness and other difficult situations, or even to die by suicide, after their divorce.*[12] In fact, most divorced fathers are extremely lonely, overwrought and disoriented. This is a consequence of having lost connection, daily contact with their children. With the loss of daily engagement with their children many men become disconnected from their sense of purpose and passion in life.

---

[2] Kposowa A.J. (2003) "Divorce and Suicide Risk Journal of Epidemiology & Community Health; 57: 993.

There are some qualitive conclusions that suggests that women who did not have a secure, loving relationship with her own parents while she was growing up are more likely to be overly indulgent and overly submissive in raising her own children, regardless of their income, education or marital status. This could be because they're trying to compensate for parental wounding in their own childhood.

Men, it's difficult to come to this conclusion, but the reality is that when you are absent from the home, you have abdicated your right to define your relationship with your kids, mother and your children on your terms. This is why it's so important for us to be clear on our mission and our values; that way our choices and your behavior reflect it.

Again, in the Scripture, we have this directive, *"Husbands...be considerate as you live with your wives."[13]* Guys, I think there's some important things for us to consider as we work together and partner together in raising our children with your children's mother, whether she's your spouse or your ex. If it's your ex, there are some things you're going to have to consider about her current status in life. One issue that must be considered is what was the relationship with her parents? Was it healthy? Is it challenging? What are some of the issues that you need to be aware of, because those things are going to get transferred over to you? You need to be able to understand how she feels about the divorce. Does she feel guilty? Does she feel hurt? Does she still feel rejected? Does she still

[13] 1 Peter 3:7 (NIV) also (CEV) "If you are a husband, you should be thoughtful of your wife."

As a father, you have been cut to fit specifically into the lives of those members of your family.

feel anger? You need to consider her employment situation, the ability for her to provide the kind of security she wants her kids to be able to have. You need to understand her life responsibilities, the obligations that she has, both to her finances and other relationships in her life, if you're living with your kids.

Now, if you are husband and wife living together, raising your children, here are some things you need to consider in the relationship: Is your relationship secure? Does your wife feel safe? Does she consider you to be someone trustworthy, a partner who carries an equal load with her? Do you understand what her needs are emotionally, financially, relationally? Are the household responsibilities shared, or does too much of it weigh on one of you? Most importantly, is there anything undone, commitment met, or responsibility not fulfilled?

As men, we like to give ourselves credit for our intentions, but we're actually judged by whether or not we fulfill our obligations. Those things hinder our ability to partner and to have the influence in raising and producing the kind of children who grow up feeling self-confident and who are aware and relate well to others.

The consequences of divorce increase the challenges parents face. As Fritz shared in his story, there's a stark difference between children raised in a home with both birth parents and the emotional impact of being split between two households. For those who are separated from their kids' mothers, here are some suggestions on ways you can begin to rebuild that relationship. Number one, you need to honor her as your children's mother. This is not to say that this will be easy because there's probably some inner conflict. There's likely some challenges that remain unresolved, because that's what may have contributed to the disintegration of the relationship originally. Often, mom will control how you relate to your kids. Your responsibility is to adjust the way you relate to her, so that you can do your best job as a father.

> Husbands...
> be considerate
> as you live with
> your wives.

WHAT MAKES A FAMILY

Now, if you are living with your wife, you need to understand that you and her were a family before you added kids, and that's why that relationship between husband and wife needs to be the priority. **Guys, don't forget you are a husband first, and a dad second.** When your kids see you honor their mom, treating her with respect and value, it gives them a sense of security. It validates the other half of who they are.

Let's leave with this thought found in the scripture. It says *"all of you be submissive to one another and be clothed with humility, for God resists the proud but gives grace to the humble."*[14] The Greek word translated as "submit" is "hupotasso." It doesn't just mean to come under authority or describe a

---

[14] 1 Peter 5:5 (NKJV)

hierarchy. One of the ways it was also used was to describe a puzzle piece that's been cut and designed to fit in a specific spot. And when that puzzle piece is placed in where it has been cut for, it "submits" to all of the other pieces around it. There's a process for us to understand that, **as a dad, you have been cut to fit specifically into the lives of those members of your family.** When you're missing, it leaves a hole; the picture is unfinished, and your sense of connectedness and purpose is lost.

But when everything is in its place, everyone and everything is connected and the picture of becoming the father you desire to be starts to take shape.

REFLECTION
Questions ★ ★ ★

1 The chapter states that *mothers cultivate compassion, comfort, and cooperation* while *fathers create courage, competence, and confidence*. Have there been moments when you felt the need to compete with, rather than cooperate with, the child's mother? What was the underlying concern, and how could you shift toward a partnership mindset?

2 How can you and the child's mother intentionally work together to bring out the best in your child? What is one practical step you can take to better support her role while also embracing your own?

3 Reflect on a recent interaction with your child. Was it "life giving?" If you could redo that moment, what would you do differently?

4 How does your current daily or weekly routine reflect your priorities as a father? What small adjustments could you make to be more present and engaged?

HOME
WORK

Identify a Distraction

Write down one major distraction (e.g., work, technology, stress) that takes away from your fatherhood engagement. Develop a plan to reduce its impact for one week and reflect on the results.

THE DISTRACTION

THE PLAN

Understand Her Needs

Reflect on what the child's mother needs from you to feel supported as a co-parent. Write down three things you think she values most in your role as a father. Then, ask her directly what she needs from you. Compare the lists—what did you get right? What surprised you?

1 _____

2 _____

3 _____

WHAT SHE NEEDS FROM YOU

_____

_____

_____

Identify a Shared Goal

Parenting works best when both parents align on key values
and goals. Write down one parenting challenge or decision you need to work
through together. How can you approach it in a way that strengthens teamwork
rather than creating tension?

ONE PARENTING CHALLENGE

THE NEW APPROACH

CHAPTER 02

Show Appreciation

Write a short note (or express verbally) something you appreciate about how

the child's mother parents. Notice her strengths and acknowledge them.

Reflect on how this changes the dynamic between you both.

Sean

I discovered that being a father wasn't just about providing for my family; it was about being present.

My upbringing was shaped by the presence of a strong father and a caring yet tough mother. For my sisters and me, **Dad chose to be a father figure who was feared and respected first.** He carried an air of authority in our home, ensuring discipline and structure, but at the end of the day, his love for us was undeniable. He would do anything to help us achieve our dreams. He always was the first person our extended family called when they faced challenges, despite the occasional harsh response. Through him, I learned the importance of respect in the home. But I also learned something else—where I needed to bring more empathy and understanding into my own parenting journey.

When our first little girl was born, I quickly realized that my life was no longer my own. The days of thinking only of myself or doing what I wanted whenever I pleased were over. Parenting isn't about taking the easy route; in fact, it's quite the opposite. I discovered that being a father wasn't just about providing for my family; it was about being present. It was about slowing down, creating memories, and forming connections that would last a lifetime.

I had to learn to stop rushing through life, moving from one task to another. Instead, I learned to pause, take a breath, and cherish playtime after work. **What seemed like small moments became the foundation of my relationship with my daughter.** Those moments meant everything to her, and they became everything to me too.

Dad Academy was so helpful in helping me reflect on my values and understand the kind of father I want to be. We all have morals and principles that guide us, but they only become useful in parenting when we take the time to lay them out and truly understand what drives us as men. **Fatherhood requires a plan, a vision for our families that sets our children up for success—not just in life but as people.**

As a fairly new father, connecting with other dads through Dad Academy was a game-changer for me. Hearing their experiences, sharing struggles, and learning from men who had walked this path before me gave me the tools I needed to become the best father I could be. I know the impact of being an intentional, present, and faith-focused, values-driven dad will ripple through my children's lives for years to come. And for that, I am forever grateful.

CHAPTER

03

Destiny Destinations

Choosing Your Parenting Path

"

We all set out to make
a difference in the world.
But the first step is to
achieve the less lofty goal
of changing your
own world.

T.D. JAKES

DESTINY DECISIONS

Choosing Your Parenting Path

By now, we're discovering that being a dad is making choices based on a set of values, determining what's important, and knowing your choices are based on your values. Every decision you make is two decisions. The decision to do something is a decision not to do something else. In chapter 1 we referenced a Bible story with a character named Joshua. Joshua was the successor to Moses. While Moses led the people out of slavery, it was Joshua's job to lead them into their future. At a critical moment in their journey, Joshua says to the people he has led and served, *"If serving the Lord seems undesirable to you, then choose for yourself this day whom you will serve, whether the gods of your ancestors, that your ancestors served beyond the Euphrates (in the past) or the gods of the Amorites in whose land you're living (in the present). But as for me and my house, we're going to serve the Lord."* [15] Every man makes choices. Sometimes we lose sight of the fact that our choices have an impact on everyone entrusted to our care. **That's why it is important to make choices that are driven by our values.** How you make those decisions determines your success in fulfilling your mission.

---

[15] Joshua 24:15 (NKJV)

TREES OR TUMBLEWEEDS?

Children do what they see. If what you saw growing up wasn't healthy, or if you live with residual pain from your childhood, it influences your capacity to fulfill your mission. It is important that every father parent proactively, not reactively, so that we can be intentional and not just parent by default. What do I mean by default? Default is our programming; I call it our emotional muscle memory.

Neurologists have been able to take pictures of our brain and are able to see how different thoughts activate our brain and its internal wiring. The stimulus travels along neural pathways, and by following these pathways - they begin to fire in our brain. Imagine with me a picture of a tree with a thick trunk and healthy, long branches. This is what healthy thought patterns or brain function looks like.

Now imagine with me a tumbleweed, one that's all tangled and turned back into itself. That is what a toxic thought, like fear or worry or anxiety, looks like. When you consider the two images **one can see how our thoughts are a matter of life or death.** You can see how healthy thinking produces a clear, organized, uncluttered mind. On the other hand, toxic thinking - worry, fear, doubt, anger, unforgiveness - keeps us tangled in our own dysfunction.

The way we think, and what we think about, determines the experience that we call life; it shapes us more than we have ever realized. If this is true, there's some good news for you: we can actually renew our minds. We're designed to be able to rewire our brain. Thanks to something called neuroplasticity **you can write new neural pathways that can actually overwrite all the bad programming that has accumulated through our lives.**

A WHOLE NEW WORLD

In fact, this is exactly what Scripture tells us to do. In his letter to the church in Rome, the apostle Paul says, *"And don't be conformed to this world, but be transformed by the renewing of your mind, that you may prove what is that good, acceptable and perfect will of God."* [16] This Greek word for world ("aión") describes the way that you think and feel, your process and your perspective. The "world" we tend to conform to is the one that we've created for ourselves, the one that explains me to me. For example, it's the abused person who always processes life through the filter of pain. It's the lonely or rejected individual that is always on the defensive because of their need for self-preservation, or the overachiever who always needs to prove something.

> The best dads parent proactively, not reactively.

These are examples of the world that we conform to, the choices that we make, the behavior we exhibit based on something we value, or of an experience that has shaped our perspective on life. Like the picture of those toxic thought

---

[16] Romans 12:2 (NKJV)

tumbleweeds, our feelings and processes are all tangled up in these past experiences, and the more we yield to it, the more they become integrated in the way we view ourselves and the world around us. We truly are a product of our world.

If we want to have a different "world," we have to be able to let go of the past. One Scripture reminds us how important it is to do this in the book Hebrews. *The author of this letter says we must get rid of everything that slows us down, especially the sin that distracts us.*[17] We must run the race that lies ahead of us and never give up. So we're going to look at three issues from our past that can hinder us from being the dad that we want to be.

> The "world" we tend to conform to is the one that we've created for ourselves,
> the one that explains me to me.

LOOKING BACK AT DAD[18]

The first wound from our past is our own relationship with our dad. We've talked about how important dad is. The problem is, I don't think all dads understand how important they actually are. Most men don't have the skill or the emotional intelligence to deal with their own emotional baggage. Whether it's intentional or not, we tend to push our stuff on our kids.

---

[17] Hebrews 12:1
[18] These concepts were inspired by Men's Fraternity: The Quest for Authentic Manhood by Dr. Robert Lewis (2005) LifeWay Church Resources.

When you have a wound in your heart from Dad, it results in a couple of unhealthy behaviors. The first is that we have unhealthy emotions because our life is rooted in anger and pain. When dad is not around, kids are frustrated. They're fearful because they have no one to provide them with the courage and heart that they need for life.

They grow up without a sense of competence and the confidence that they can handle what life throws at them. **As a result, children lose heart.** They internalize the pain, and they end up hurting others. Maybe that's some of your story, similar to some of the profiles of the men included in the book. As a man takes a look at his center, the values that direct his life, there's some dysfunction that may be a product of what was missing from his childhood.

Another obstacle is *unhealthy behaviors* that are revealed in *addictions and obsessions*. That's why men find ways to escape from life. We pursue things that produce the feel-good chemicals in our brain. For some guys it's numbing out through alcohol or drugs or medication. For others, it is drowning the pain out by participating in risky behaviors that trigger the fight or flight instincts. Unfortunately, that approach is only a distraction from addressing our pain. Some men become obsessed with being noticed, trying to make dad proud. Either way, take note: Anger and fear are how pain is expressed. Addiction is how pain is suppressed.

The way we think, and what we think about, determines the experience that we call life; it shapes us more than we have ever realized.

We have to be able to go deep inside of ourselves, to look ourselves in the mirror, to identify those places of pain and begin to develop a healthy new perspective. It is not just a new perspective on what had happened or what our childhood lacked, but on a change that we need to make - a renewing of our mind so that we can be the dad that we want to be.

MEMORIES OF MOM[19]

When a dad is absent or distant, it creates another wound, and that's with mom. Let's talk about four types of wounded moms who inadvertently have a negative impact on their children. You may have witnessed one of these moms in your own childhood. The first type is the *ignorant mom*. They just don't know what they don't know, so they become overly involved. In time, she evolves into a suffocating mom that never lets their kids grow up, especially boys. They're the mom that's always making food for you, that wakes you up for school and makes your bed. It comes from a desire to express care and concern for their children, but it actually blocks their growth and ability to embrace responsibility. Because their identity is tied up in the role of nurturing and creating security, they often struggle to create healthy boundaries.

There's also the *insecure* or *needy mom*. This is the one who unknowingly uses her kids to fill the emotional gap that she's missing in her own life. She's insecure and doesn't have anyone to come alongside her. That's why she tends to measure her worth by the affection and the attention that comes from her children.

[19] Ibid.

The third type is the *injured mom*, the controlling mom for whom everything is a battle for power in the family. It's a battle for loyalty, because she's been hurt, and she's trying to make sure that that kind of pain never happens again. She's always going to make sure he has the upper hand.

Lastly, there's the *intervening mom*. This is the "do it all mom", the one who feels the pressure to be both mom and dad. Unfortunately, in our world, too many moms have been forced into this type of condition. She does it all, sacrificing everything for the sake of her children. The problem is she often pays the price personally, much later on in life. All of this attention, all of this affirmation, all of this opportunity, looks like love and caring, but we don't even realize that it really comes from a place of fear in their lives. Oftentimes needing or exerting control in situations and in relationships is how fear is expressed in an individual's life.

> **Anger and fear are how pain is expressed. Addiction is how pain is suppressed.**

As you think about the outcome of your relationship with your mother please remember: she did her best to give you her best.

THE LONELY LIFE[20]

The third kind of wound that a man may have to face is the feeling of being

---

deserted and all alone. It's a result of having to navigate life without any healthy mentoring relationships. **It's like missing the relational capital you need to build your life.** As a result, we start all of our relationships from a deficit, a social, emotional, and spiritual deficit. This disadvantage to life produces three results: loneliness because we live and have learned to navigate our life in isolation without really any kind of authentic connection and someone who knows us.

It also produces *foolishness* in our life. **Foolishness is really just the product of our isolation.** It's the feeling that the only person that we have to go to, or that we trust, is ourselves. The problem with being isolated is knowing that we don't always make the right decisions, knowing that we don't always process correctly, because our processor might be broken, and we find ourselves making mistakes that could have easily been avoided had we had someone else to rely on.

The final consequence of the all-alone world are the blind spots that develop in our life. They're things that we don't see about ourselves, things that we don't recognize. Because we can't see them, we continue to develop these shortcomings. Over time, they are reinforced and continue to do damage in our life. Not having someone in our lives to alert us to our flaws is detrimental to a man's success in life. These relationships are important not to focus on our failures, but to help us see the things that we can't see about ourselves.

Not having someone in our lives to alert us to our flaws is detrimental to a man's success in life.

Without other significant relationships in our lives, we'll just keep making wrecks of things and relationships. It's kind of like what the writer of Proverbs says, *some people think they're doing right, but in the end, it leads to death.* [21]

Remember the picture of those thoughts we see here? Why? What? How we think about our parenting is all tangled up. That's why we need a reprogramming. And the reprogramming of our brain and of our heart begins with making new choices based on new values in week one, where we said that we're going to start to realize that being a dad is: 1) making choices based on a set of values and 2) determining what is truly important.

Remember, every decision we make is two decisions. The decision to do something is also the choice not to do something else. I want to encourage you to choose to begin to renew your mind. *Again, we turn to the ancient wisdom found in Proverbs: as a man thinks in his heart, so is he.*[22] If you want to be able to make new choices, we have to be able to think differently. And to think differently, we have to relearn how not to conform anymore to the world we've created and rewire our way of thinking that reflects our values and life's purpose. If we don't, our past becomes a weight that slows us and drags us down. If we are able to address these issues in our lives, we won't pass on our handicaps to our kids, we'll refuse to impose our woundedness on them. It will free you to be able to create new pathways of health and wholeness that we're able to pass on to the people around us.

---

[21] Proverbs 14:12
[22] Proverbs 23:7

REFLECTION
Questions ★ ★ ★

1 What values from your own upbringing (good or bad) have influenced your current parenting style? How do they align with the values you want to pass on to your children?

2 The chapter discusses "emotional muscle memory" and how past wounds shape our behavior. What are some thought patterns or reactions you recognize in yourself that may be rooted in past experiences?

3 In what ways have past relationships with your own parents shaped your expectations and challenges in co-parenting?

4 If you could change one negative mindset or behavior that affects your parenting, what would it be? What steps can you take to start that change?

HOME
WORK

Reflect on Your Childhood Home

Write down one word that describes how your childhood home felt to you. Then, write a few sentences explaining why you chose that word. What do you want to replicate or change in your own home?

HOW YOUR CHILDHOOD HOME FELT

WHAT TO REPLICATE OR CHANGE

Identify Thought Patterns

Take a few minutes to write down three recurring thoughts you have about yourself as a father. Are these thoughts rooted in truth, or are they shaped by past experiences? If they are negative or limiting, rewrite them into positive, intentional statements.

Break the Cycle

Identify one specific behavior or reaction in your parenting that you feel is shaped by past wounds. Write down an alternative response that reflects the father you want to be.

ONE BEHAVIOUR THAT'S SHAPED BY PAST WOUNDS

ALTERNATE RESPONSE

Strengthen Your Support System

Think about the people in your life who can serve as mentors or accountability partners in your fatherhood journey. Write down one or two names and set a goal to reach out for support, wisdom, or guidance this week.

1 _____

2 _____

3 _____

HOW WILL YOU REACH OUT THIS WEEK?

_____

_____

_____

I am committed to being present, to learning, and to supporting other dads as we navigate this journey together.

When my parents divorced when I was three, my stepfather, "Pops," entered my life—a true blessing and miracle. My childhood was filled with simple joys and invaluable lessons. He didn't just teach me values through words; he lived them. He embodied the principles he wanted to impart, showing me what it meant to be a man of integrity, love, and selflessness. The most selfless thing he ever did was marry my mother without knowing my sister and me, yet he embraced us as his own without hesitation. He never had biological children of his own, but that never mattered—he was a true hero to us. For his love and acceptance, I will always be grateful.

Looking back, I see how much of the man I am today is because of his influence. I've needed to lean on that experience as I navigate fatherhood and the realities of a blended family. **As a father, stepfather, and husband, balancing professional growth while remaining present for my family has been one of my greatest challenges.** The complexities of a blended family, especially one striving to honor God, add another layer to the journey. I quickly learned that there's a stark difference between natural child development and the emotional impact of being split between two homes. Then, add the digital era, where instant gratification often replaces the ability to work through emotions like sadness, anxiety, and pressure. Our culture glamorizes success but often ignores the struggle that comes with it. **Recognizing and supporting my children's emotional needs as they evolve into unique individuals has been an incredible learning experience.** This journey pushes me to keep adapting, growing, and striving to be the best father I can be.

Participating in Dad Academy has been a transformative experience in my journey as a father. Through Dad Academy, I've discovered the power of active listening—putting aside distractions to genuinely connect with my kids and my fellow fathers. This has strengthened my relationships and deepened my appreciation for shared experiences. I've also learned the importance of vulnerability. By encouraging my kids and other dads to express their emotions and seek help when needed, we've built an environment of trust and support. Tackling tough conversations together has reinforced a culture that values both personal well-being and strong parenting.

Fathers are essential in today's world, and we need each other now more than ever. I am committed to being present, to learning, and to supporting other dads as we navigate this journey together. **Fatherhood isn't just a role— it's a calling, and I want to make the most of it.**

04

Developing Character

Building Trust and
Cultivating Courage

"

My father gave me the greatest gift anyone could give another person...

He believed in me.

JIM VALVANO

DEVELOPING CHARACTER

Building Trust and Cultivating Courage

*T*here are three things dads are responsible to help to develop in kids: They develop a kid's courage, competency and confidence. These are critical skills for them to have as we prepare them for life. Let's begin by starting with courage because *courage reflects character.*

Character provides the infrastructure our children will depend upon for the rest of their lives. Strong character is what makes our children good employees, good friends, good teammates, good citizens, good spouses, and ultimately, good parents themselves. It is one thing to know the right thing to do; it's another thing to actually do the right thing. It's courage, having an internal strength that gets it done.

DEFINING COURAGE

There are many definitions of courage. Bethany Hamilton, the one-armed, professional surfer and subject of the feature film "Soul Surfer" says, "Courage doesn't mean that you don't get afraid. Courage means that you don't let fear

---

¹⁵ Joshua 24:15 (NKJV)

stop you." The actual definition for courage comes from its root word. The root word for courage is the Latin word "*cor*", which means strength of heart. It is an inner strength, the ability to face difficult things, to confront one's own limitations. It gives one the ability to live life being "all in."

For our purposes in Dad Academy, let's use this definition: **courage is how trust or faith responds to risk**. As a parent it's easy in that sentence to focus on the word "risk," but it's not the key word because life is always going to be filled with challenges with opportunities. Our job is to help them learn to evaluate what is in front of them and to be able to respond with courage. Our job is not to prevent our kids from experiencing difficulty. It is to make sure that they have the heart to endure it and to come out better for it on the other side.

> Our job is not to prevent our kids from experiencing difficulty. It is to make sure that they have the heart to endure it and to come out better for it on the other side.

When my kids were little they loved being in the water. It didn't matter if it was the pool or the ocean, they couldn't get enough. They were good as long as they could touch the bottom. I remember when they were learning to swim, I would stand in the deep end near the side of the pool, extend my arms and invite them to jump to me. At first they would hesitantly walk to the edge. Then, they'd have to choose whether to jump or stay where they were safe. They had to decide whether they would trust what they knew about the water, or trust what they knew about me. Eventually, they jumped. It was hard the first time, but it soon became one of their favorite things to do when we were around the water, because they knew they could trust dad to catch them.

The key to developing courage is developing the skill of trust. Can I trust myself? Can I trust the information that has been provided to me? Can I trust my experience? So, a dad creates self-confidence and skills by teaching them how to trust. He does this by being someone who is trustworthy, reliable and truthful.

CULTIVATING CHARACTER

Now this is where we start getting into character. See, you are the mirror your kids look into. **If you were to take a moment for reflection, what do you see? Do you see yourself living out the character qualities you want them to have? What do they see about your life? Are there qualities in your life that you want replicated in them?**

Your Turn

If you're like most dads, you have a list of personal shortcomings that we don't want to pass on to our children. . But we need to find the best parts of us and model them so they can become the best qualities in them. As that happens, we will also help to draw out the unique qualities that God has placed in them.

What are some things that make for good character in a person we've already talked about? For example, *reliability*. You must ask yourself: Can other people depend on you? Can you teach your kids how to be dependable? Jesus even talks about how this character trait is developed: *If you are faithful with a little, you'll eventually be trusted with more.*[23] Part of cultivating trust in our children requires providing them with things that they can succeed in, so that they will be prepared to take on new and greater responsibilities.

> **Fatherhood involves teaching your children that life isn't just about themselves, but about developing a commitment to the greater good.**

Another issue related to trust is loyalty. *Loyalty* is another skill that's cultivated over time. It involves teaching your children life isn't just about themselves, but about developing a commitment to the greater good. It's the attentiveness not only to other's needs and desires, but having the determination to stick in and

[23] Luke 16:10

stick it out with people, no matter what they go through. This is especially true for those with whom you have a responsibility and obligation.

A third dimension of trust is *honesty* or truthfulness. Being truthful, especially about one's self, is the ability to acknowledge one's strengths and weaknesses, to differentiate between the good and the bad, the helpful and the detrimental. The skill of truthfulness is having a perspective on life that allows you to process the correct information and apply faith to it. That's what truthfulness really is. It's taking the available information and applying faith as a filter, so you can make a determination about how to respond to people and situations with courage.

The last issue is *integrity*. **Integrity is anchored in the concept of wholeness and strength.** When we say that a person has integrity, it is a compliment to the consistency of their character. But when the word integrity is applied to a building, it refers to the fact that the structure is strong due to the manner of its construction and the way the various elements of the structure are tied into each other. "Integrated" and "integrity" come from the same root: "integer" which is defined as "a complete entity, whole". It's a Latin word that means "untouched" and "undivided". Integrity is really about how our life is integrated and connected so that one's life has strength and stability. It's important to understand that choices and behavior are reflective of our values; we need to make sure that our values are integrated in our life and in our behavior.

Integrity is how our values are integrated and connected in everyday life so that one's life has strength and stability.

These traits - reliability, loyalty, honesty, integrity - how are they developed in a person's life? They're developed through discipline.

MORE IS CAUGHT THAN TAUGHT

Discipline is not a negative word. It is not punishment. Discipline actually comes from the word "disciple", which means to teach or to train. I want to point to another verse in the Bible. It says, *"Train up a child in the way that he should go, and when he's old, he will not depart from it."* Another translation says, *Teach children in a way that fits their needs.*[24] And even when they're old, they will not leave the right path.   Dad, we're back to the important responsibility we have to train our children. In training your children, you teach them how to trust you as their teacher and example.

Training has so much to do, not just with doing, but with being - who you are and how you live. It's said that "more is caught than taught". They will learn more from what they observe from you more than from what you tell them. When they learn what is important from seeing how you live, they're going to learn to embrace those values. Because training teaches them what is important. Discipline shows them the values that we're going to live by.

Take a look again at the verse we just referenced. We have to remember that training each one of your children is going to be individualized. Because it is based on their specific needs, it is not one size fits at all. While values are

[24] Proverbs. 22:6 (ERV)

universal, they'll be applied differently. Every child deserves the blessing of Dad's personal attention and personalized training.

DETERMINING BOUNDARIES

Training also requires boundaries. Freedom really comes from having limitations, knowing where your boundaries are. Let me explain it this way: some boundaries in our life are for security. Like a boundary is to make sure that you look both ways before you cross the street, or as they take on more responsibility, not texting while driving. **Teaching boundaries helps us learn how to define risk,** which builds reliability. Can I trust the information? Can I evaluate it? Can I make an informed decision about what I need to do?

Boundaries provide structure. They keep things orderly and moving, like traffic. This is another way boundaries build integrity, because we begin to see how things connect together and function for the benefit of others as well as for one's self.

Lastly, boundaries define success. Everyone who plays a game knows games have rules; the rules tell us what is permissible and what is not. Sometimes the rules of life can be complicated like some sports. A few years ago, I had some first-generation immigrant neighbors come to my home to watch the World Series. They had no experience with baseball, except for knowing "three strikes and you're out." But even that concept is complicated. A strike could be a pitch that is not swung at, but crosses over home plate. It could also be a pitch that it swung at and missed. It could also be a foul ball that is hit but does not land within the field of play (except on the third strike for which a foul ball allows the batter to remain at bat). Good thing my neighbors also knew about the "home run," a ball that never touches the ground within the field of play, but allows the batter and any runners on base to score. Baseball, like life, can be complicated. But when you understand the rules and know how success will be measured, you at least know how to approach winning. Boundaries help us teach our kids what success and winning feel like, because they understand the rules that define the responsibility that leads to victory.

CONFRONTING AND COMPLIMENTING

Finally, training requires consequences, both positive and negative. There's a lot of information about different ways or methods to discipline or not discipline children. When my wife and I were raising our children, who are now adults, we decided that we were going to focus our **discipline by not only correcting behavior that was not in line with our family's values, we also wanted to commend behavior that was reflective of our family values.** We determined that we were going to confront disobedience in our children's lives. If they just rebelled and didn't do what was asked of them, then that was something that needed to be addressed.

Because we value truthfulness and honesty, we chose to confront deceitfulness. Lying, blaming others, and general dishonesty were going to cause them problems down the road.

And because honor is a value in our home, we said that we're going to confront disrespect. We informed them that they may not agree with every decision in the home. Other times they may have found certain requests or expectations easy to comply with. Regardless of their feelings at the moment we did not want disrespect to shape our responses to one another. Over the years there were disagreements, but because we value relationships and value the uniqueness of each individual, we held kids accountable for personal attacks and dishonoring another.

Deceitfulness, Dishonesty, Disrespect - these were the attitudes and behaviors that received corrective attention in our home. But even as we confronted wrong behavior, we also chose to reinforce and reward behavior we wanted to see repeated. We complimented *thoughtfulness* whenever they put other people first. We complimented *thankfulness* in their lives, because we value gratitude. And we complimented *truthfulness* so that they would be people who are true to themselves and to who God is shaping them to be.

VALUES BASED DISCIPLINE

As parents, my wife and I were determined to affirm our kids when we

saw something we wanted them to repeat. We didn't just affirm their achievements or their talents, we affirmed their character. We drew special attention to behaviors that demonstrated that they were becoming who they could and they should be. **As a dad, I developed a discipline myself; I used to watch and try to catch my kids doing something right. I wanted them to know dad wasn't only their biggest fan outside, but that he was always watching and wanted to cheer them on when they were doing the right thing at the right time,** knowing that it would build courage in their heart.

As a dad, have you ever thought about what you are going to compliment in your kid's life? What are you going to correct or confront in their lives? How you do either of these things is extremely important. One of the things that we try to live by is this simple saying: *praise in public, correct in private.* Our approach was to compliment the behavior that reflected our family values

> **Praise in public, correct in private.**

publicly in front of others, but that we would confront or correct the wrong behavior in private. We had a goal for the training or discipling that we gave our children. **We would help develop character and courage in their lives by establishing clear boundaries, not just rules and regulations, but also recognition and reward for demonstrating good character based on our family's values and in their individual uniqueness.** We understood our

Courage is an inner strength that gives a person the ability to live life being "all in."

mission, because we had a goal in sight, and we identified our values which centered us. By reinforcing these values, we hoped they would be able to embrace them as well and cultivate them in their own lives

THINGS COURAGEOUS PEOPLE SAY

There's a way that courageous people talk. I think there are three simple phrases courageous people say. The first one is *"thank you."* Children need to know they are not going to be able to navigate life without help. Asking for that help is tremendously courageous. Acknowledging the simple actions of others is not just considerate, but it also reflects one's gratitude. Courageous people also say the flipside of that coin. Not only do they say thank you, but they also say *"you're welcome."* It's more than simple courtesy or politeness. It's an acknowledgement of the other party's appreciation. This reply also assures them that they are under no obligation to return the favor.

> There are four simple phrases courageous people say:
> "Thank you."
> "You're welcome."
> "I'm sorry."
> "I forgive you."

Courageous people are able to say, *"I'm sorry."* They're able to admit when they were wrong. Of all the things I could have done better as a father, apologizing to my children is one thing I really tried to do well. I didn't try to maintain an image of a perfect dad, just one who was in process. I believe them seeing me acknowledge my mistakes and transgressions demonstrate that I was still growing and changing for the better. In a culture that prefers blaming others or making excuses, taking personal responsibility demonstrates character and integrity. In the same way, courageous people say, *"I forgive you."* It releases the other person from the threat that their actions will be held against them or used against them at a future time. Responses like "it's no big deal" are insufficient because if it wasn't a big deal, the person wouldn't have felt the need to admit their trespass. *"I forgive you"* releases them and you from any relational debt.

BEING A COURAGEOUS DAD

There are three things courageous fathers say. *"I love you"* expresses your commitment to your children. *"I'm proud of you"* affirms their character. And *"you're good at…"* communicates that they have your attention, that you see them, and commend them for the effort they give towards developing their God-given gifts and abilities and pressing through challenges.

Disciplining our children is less about correcting them and more about bringing out the promise and the potential that God has placed inside of them.

We desire to raise children who have the courage to confront risks in their lives, knowing that hardship or trouble or tribulation does not derail them, but it helps to build them and shape them in the process. **Kids who have character are going to be courageous people.** Remember, courage is defined as how trust responds to risk. If kids grow up trusting their model (you, dad) and they can trust their training, they won't have anything to prove to anyone and they can attack life with courage.

REFLECTION
Questions ★ ★ ★

1 Think of a time when your child faced a challenge—did they trust themselves, the process, or you? How did your response impact their confidence?

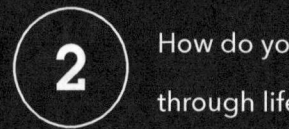

How do you show your child that they can trust you to guide them through life's challenges? In what ways do you help your child learn to trust themselves and their decision-making abilities?

3 Do you correct behavior based on your values, or do you find yourself reacting emotionally? Do your methods reinforce trust and courage, or do they create fear and insecurity? How can you ensure discipline reinforces character rather than just punishing behavior?

HOME
WORK

1 Write down the behaviors that violate your family's values and need to be corrected ("confront"). Write down the behaviors that demonstrate your family's values and should be reinforced with affirmation ("compliment"). Commit to intentionally correcting and complimenting these behaviors throughout the week.

CONFRONT

COMPLIMENT

2 Write down some of the boundaries and guidelines that have been established for your children. How do the boundaries you set for your child help them feel secure and build confidence? Are there any boundaries that need to be redefined and/or clarified?

_____

_____

_____

_____

_____

_____

_____

3 Make a commitment to say "I love you," "I'm proud of you," and "You're good at…" to your child this week.

I swallowed my pride and went to my dad for help.

Ten dimes. I can still picture them stacked neatly on our kitchen table as my parents explained what an allowance was. A whole dollar! As a young boy, I had no idea I was about to receive my first lesson in stewardship. My parents laid it out clearly: if I did all my chores for the week, I would receive ten dimes every Saturday. If I didn't, no dimes. The other condition? One of those dimes had to go with me to church the next day.

"But I get to keep the other nine?" I asked, wide-eyed. "What a deal!" As I got older, allowances turned into part-time jobs, and the concept of "tithing,"[25] giving 10% of my paycheck was never difficult—it was just what I had always done. I still got to keep most of what I earned. **But when real-life responsibilities hit, I found myself struggling financially for the first time.** My paycheck didn't stretch far enough, and I started wondering if that 10% could help me cover some of my growing expenses. So, I stopped tithing.

Unfortunately, my financial struggles only deepened. Bills piled up, and I felt completely overwhelmed. Finally, I swallowed my pride and went to my dad for help. He had always managed his finances wisely, and I had watched him do so with discipline over the years. Sitting at the kitchen table

---

[24] Tithing (the word "tithe" means "tenth") is concept found in the Bible. It is a practical way that one 1) Honors God by expressing gratitude for God's blessing and generosity; 2) Demonstrates trust in God's ability to provide for your needs; and, 3) Puts God first in your life and finances. (Proverbs 3:9-10; Malachi 3:9-10) The purpose of tithing is to teach you to always put God first in your lives." Deuteronomy 14:23 (TLB)

once again, we went through every bill and debt I had accumulated. **He didn't get angry. He didn't lecture me.** Instead, he pulled out his checkbook and started writing checks to clear my debts.

He rescued me that day—but not without a cost. He made it clear that I would pay him back, and together, we created a plan to do just that. It took me a few years, but I repaid every penny. The biggest condition he gave me? Tithing was no longer optional. I had to trust God with my finances. Since that day, I have lived credit card debt-free and have never missed an opportunity to tithe. My dad was still teaching me, even as an adult.

When I started thinking about My Dad Plan, I knew financial stewardship was something I wanted to pass down to my kids. But until then, I hadn't been intentional about starting. Dad Academy gave me the structure to take all of the ideas, traditions, and lessons that had been floating around in my head and put them into action.

Following Dad Academy, we implemented an allowance system in our home—four dollars and four quarters (because, you know, inflation). **I am grateful for a father who not only taught me as a child but continues to lead me as a man.** And I am thankful for Dad Academy, which has helped me craft a plan to raise children with courage, competency, and confidence.

CHAPTER

05

Creating Competency

Preparing Kids For Life

"A (child) needs a father to show (them) how to be in the world... (They) need to be taught how to read a map so that they can recognize the roads that lead to life and the paths that lead to death. How to know what love requires. And where to find steel in the heart when life makes demands on us that are greater than we think we can endure."

IAN MORGAN CRON

CREATING COMPETENCY

Preparing Kids for Life

*W*hen I was around eleven or twelve years old, my grandparents came from the Midwest to visit us in what was, at that time, a relatively small town on the central coast of California. My dad had been teaching me how to drive a car, first by sitting on his lap and letting me steer and eventually letting me get in the driver's seat to drive around an empty parking lot. Now in that parking lot I gained some experience with starting and stopping, even working the manual drive having learned how to use the clutch and stick shift.

As my Dad and I were coming home from the grocery store, we saw down the block that our whole family, including my visiting grandparents, uncle and aunt, was gathered in the front yard. I remember begging my Dad to let me drive the final block home so to show everyone my new skill. So, he allowed me to scoot over to the driver's seat. I was so proud to show off my driving skills and doing great until I had to make a right turn to pull the VW Beetle into the driveway. I overshot the turn a little, and with everyone watching I got a little nervous.

Instead of putting the car in reverse and backing up to get a better angle, I panicked, and accidentally popped the clutch. The VW lurched forward, up the curb right and was stopped by the fire hydrant on the sidewalk. My dad and I were not injured, neither were any family members. Only the driver's side front fender and headlight suffered any damage. While I suffered a little embarrassment, the family had a good laugh, and my Dad was a good sport about repairing the car.

This story reminds me of the three things a dad develops in his children: courage, competency and confidence. As this story demonstrates, I had cultivated some courage, but my competency for that life skill and the situation hadn't yet been fully developed.

Developing courage is cultivating the heart of our children. By learning how to trust, children can learn how to become courageous, because they learn how to navigate challenges. This in turn develops their character and helps them to navigate adversity and to not let fear keep them from taking risks.

CONSTRUCTING COMPETENCE

It's time to talk about the second C of fathering: Competency. Competency is the ability to do something successfully or effectively. **We all want our kids to be able to navigate life successfully and to feel capable.** This is another side of training, which begins when our kids are little. Everything you knew how to do as a child, from making your bed to tying your shoes is a skill you had to be taught. Consider the fact that children have to be trained how to go to the bathroom. It would seem that sitting in one's own excrement would be motivation enough to learn a new way of doing things. Yet, it's funny how some kids can be so resistant to this change. Can you imagine if your child never learned this skill? Gross.

Training is teaching, and training is usually hands on. Think about some of the skills people taught you how to do. I remember the day my dad showed me how to ride a bike. Later in life, he taught me how to balance my checkbook. I remember when my grandfather showed me how to put paint on a wall. So many of the skills I have in my life, big or small, are because somebody showed me how to do it. So many things in life require someone showing us how to do something. That process of training and of learning creates an important knowledge base that we get to draw on throughout life.

There's a story of legendary UCLA men's basketball coach, John Wooden who led his teams to ten consecutive NCAA championships. He spent the first practice of every season teaching his players how to put on their socks and how to tie their shoes (back when Chuck Taylor Converse and wool socks were the top equipment available). Now, you'd think college students would know how to do this. But Coach Wooden's instruction served a much greater purpose. He didn't want them to waste time retying their shoes during a game. He didn't want them to develop the blisters that were common because of the equipment that was available back in those days. More importantly, it developed a knowledge base his team would return to over and over. The deeper knowledge he was imparting to these young men was the fact that it's the details that really make the difference. Attention to the details often determines one's ability to succeed or fail.

WHAT IS INTELLIGENCE?

This ability to acquire and to apply knowledge is what we call intelligence. If our kids are going to learn how to navigate life successfully, they're going to have to gain some intelligence. There are two ways to define intelligence. **One is the ability to apply knowledge and skills.** I have a saying that I use as a coach: "to know and not to do is not to know." Don't tell me what you know. Show me what you know by doing what you've been taught.

> Everything you knew how to do as a child, from making your bed to tying your shoes, is a skill you had to be taught.

The other kind of intelligence is **the collection of valuable information.** Think of it like how a spy is deployed to gather intelligence, collect information. Both of these are great definitions, because we understand that life requires intelligence. Intelligence is crucial for competency. And competency is what allows one to navigate life capably and successfully.

The two types of intelligence kids require are *emotional intelligence* and *experiential intelligence*, relational skills and situational skills. Emotional intelligence is the ability to understand, to express and to control one's own emotions. Everyone must learn self-regulation and have the ability to to know what kinds of emotions need to be expressed and what kinds need to be suppressed. Somewhere along the line, we learned that gratitude is better than complaining. Somewhere along the line, we discovered that being around somebody who's joyful is better than being around somebody who is grumpy. We need to be able to help our children understand how to manage their emotions and which emotions should be on display. We also need to understand what kind of emotions need to be controlled. We don't just let our kids go around throwing tantrums. It doesn't help them learn the skills of self-discipline and self-control. It's an important part of a father's job to train his children how to regulate themselves.

THE IMPORTANCE OF EMOTIONAL INTELLIGENCE

Emotional intelligence is also the ability to apply those same skills in your relationships with others. The relational skills of empathy, compassion, consideration, are ways in which we demonstrate emotional intelligence. It gives us the ability to navigate relationships.

To know and not to do, is not to know.

Without consciously thinking about it, we all understand the need for emotional intelligence. This need is identified almost as soon as a child begins to communicate with self-awareness. For example, after a child's first words (which are usually Mama or Dada), what is the next word that they learn? "Mine", right? When we teach kids to share, we're training them in emotional intelligence.

When we try to tell our teen that this new friend is not good for them and we're able to explain why we've arrived at that conclusion, we're helping them learn how to use emotional intelligence to make their own determinations. Most simply, when we teach them how to say "thank you," and "I'm sorry" (the words that courageous people are able to use), we're training them in emotional intelligence.

Why is emotional intelligence so important? To be honest, it's because so many people just don't get it. **Take a moment to think about what contributes most to a person's success in life? Is it over here on the technical skill or emotional skill, social skills?**

_____

_____

_____

Your Turn

Is it some kind of blend? Let's look at where research has landed.

Research conducted with Fortune 500 CEOs by the Stanford Research Institute International and the Carnegie Melon Foundation, found that 75% of long-term job success depends on people skills (their ability to communicate and cooperate, their ability to serve instead of lead), while only 25% on technical knowledge.[26] You know what that means? It means you get further along in the world by being considerate of and cooperating with others than you do for being smart. That's emotional intelligence.

THE ABC's OF EMOTIONAL INTELLIGENCE

So, how do dads teach emotional intelligence? I call it the ABCs. "A" is *affection*. Maybe you've been exposed to the "Five Love Languages" by Dr. Gary Chapman, PhD, a popular and powerful book we use in our own family. He suggests there are five ways people express or receive love: words of affirmation, acts of service, gifts, time, and touch. While all of these are significant, I

Kids need physical affection and verbal affection.

think it's important for fathers to understand the importance of having physical contact, providing our children with physical affection, hugs and kisses. A long-

---

[26] Cited by Ranjit S Malhi (2009) "The hard truth about graduate employability and soft skills." ADEPT: Higher Education Leadership Research Bulletin 3: 45-56.

[27] Gollwitzer, A., France, K. D., & Hitti, L. E. and A. (2024, November 27). "How a parent's affection shapes a child's happiness." SPSP. https://spsp.org/news-center/character-context-blog/how-parents-affection-shapes-childs-happiness

term study out of Duke University observed parents with their children at eight months old and measured the level of affection, from extravagant to negative, in their interactions with their children as toddlers. Those same children were evaluated thirty-four years later, and the ones who received the greatest affection as infants had the lowest levels of stress and anxiety as adults.[27] Science supports the idea that we need eight hugs a day to be healthy. Healthy physical touch releases the hormones that reduce the risk of heart disease, fight infections, and boost our immune system.

Our kids need more than just physical affection; they need verbal affection as well. Every child needs to hear these things from their dad on a regular basis: "I love you," "I'm proud of you," and "you are good at… (fill in the blank)." This is an important way to cultivate courage, to "en-courage" (literally to pour courage into) their hearts. Both sons and daughters benefit from fatherly affection because it affirms their individual identities.

For boys, it's important because it puts them in touch with their emotions in a world that says that side of their lives needs to be cut off; it's not masculine to be emotional. Yet, you aren't truly a man unless you are in touch with your heart and your soul. **Boys need to be taught to be vulnerable, compassionate, and affectionate.**

For girls, physical affection from their father fulfills their need for security and emotional connection. Research proves what happens when girls don't receive it from their father. They go looking for it and respond to the first male who is able to provide that for them. **A father's affection is a key to his daughter's feminine identity and sense of self-worth.**[28]

Even a relationship that is close, as a girl matures into womanhood those changes can interfere with the relationship with her dad. My wife experienced this. She had always been close with her father. As she entered the teen years the affectionate side began to change. She no longer wanted the physical attention. The days of "crawling up into daddy's lap" for consolation were over. There was a 21-year difference in their ages and at 15 years old, dad was just 36. This created some uncomfortable moments on "daddy-daughter dates." Why? Because many times, people asked if she was his wife. This made dinners out and spending one on one time awkward in public settings.

My wife began to pull away physically. But there was something that didn't change in their relationship. Her dad had invested into the communication side of the relationship. He built a healthy and open line of communication throughout those teen years and well into adulthood. Studies show the average girl loves to talk. We know women have more words than men. Listening

---

[28] "Father involvement provides a buffer to a variety of negative outcomes, such as early sexual initiation, teenage pregnancy, dating violence, and risky sexual behavior. In particular, when father-daughter relationships are founded on open communication, trust, and higher levels of contact, these negative outcomes are further reduced." Sibley, D. S., & Granger, K. (2019, July 15). "How fathers influence their daughters' romantic relationships." Institute for Family Studies. https://ifstudies.org/blog/how-fathers-influence-their-daughters-romantic-relationships

sometimes is all that is needed. Other times, it's when she's seeking advice.

When a father taps into that side of his daughter, even when the physical changes begin, the relationship continues to grow and thrive. We've often heard that a wife needs communication in her relationship with her husband. It feeds that emotional need in a woman's life. It helps her to be confident in who she is and unafraid to share. As a father, you can cultivate this important part of your daughter's makeup so when she marries, this area of her life is healthy. It's clear that **appropriate affection from their father is an important building block in a child's life.**

> **Conversation with your children simply boils down to this: less talking, more listening.**

The A in emotional intelligence is affection. The "B" in the ABCs is "oBservation." I know it's not really "B" (maybe the O should be silent). *Observation* - your children are watching you. They see how you respond when things are good and when things are tough. They learn how to handle their feelings by watching you handle your own. They learn about self-control, self-sacrifice, and motivation by the example you set for them. They learn how to deal with confrontation and stress by watching how you deal with it. They learn how to value others and take personal responsibility. They learn all this and more from

Wisdom is knowing what to do...

Knowledge is knowing how to do it.

observing your life. This is an important concept to keep in mind, as these are important life competencies that we must help them develop. We can conclude that we ourselves must give some attention to improving those skills in our own life.

Affection, observation, and now the "C" stands for conversation. Conversation with your children simply boils down to this: less talking, more listening. The best way to do that is just to begin to ask them these probing questions about their life. Every response could be a question that opens up a new door to their heart.

It's recorded in the Gospels[29] that people asked Jesus over 130 questions, yet he only answered three of them. More importantly, Jesus asked over 300 questions in the Gospels. Not only did he show people what to do, but most importantly, he asked a lot of questions. Why? Because people learn best when they are able to process information and develop thoughtful responses. **Asking your kid questions teaches them to process what they're feeling, to organize their thoughts, to develop systems, and to articulate and communicate what they think and what they feel.**

THE IMPORTANCE OF EXPERIENTIAL INTELLIGENCE

Kids also need *experiential intelligence*. It's about having life experience to grow from and build on. This is the ability to learn from one's own, and to learn from other people's, experience. Earlier you were asked to think about things people taught you. I guess the next question is, what are some things that we wish someone had taught us? Maybe you've identified some areas in your life, that you see some deficiencies in. In those areas we wish someone would have sat us down and walked us through those lessons. For me, I really wish somebody would have sat me down and made me learn to save and manage my money, and how to budget. That's been a difficult life skill to cultivate on my own. Thankfully there are a lot of information and tools related to financial intelligence that I've been able to put to use. Still, I wish I'd have had that information earlier in my life and someone to help me develop that skill.

As a father you have to understand that one of the primary jobs of being a father is to pass on your skills to your children. **So, the first step is to ask yourself, "what do I know how to do?"** Do I know how to make scrambled eggs? Do I know how to frame up a wall? Do I know how to change oil? Do I know how to iron clothes?

This is not about using your children as cheap labor, getting your kids to do the things you don't even want to do. But, when you invite them to learn how to do these things you know how to do, with you in a side-by-side method, then we're not only passing on helpful information to them. **What we're really doing is teaching them how to share life, to ask for help, and to learn to work with someone.** It also teaches them responsibility and helps them to develop a good work ethic. Doing tasks and learning skills alongside you also builds their sense of self-worth, because they know when they've actually accomplished something that is worth doing.

ENGAGING EXTERNAL RELATIONSHIPS

Experiential intelligence is not only about passing on what you know, but it's also about introducing your children to other significant relationships. **Have you ever considered "Who do I know that knows what I don't?"** One of the hardest things that every parent comes to realize is that there comes a time when you stop parenting by yourself. As they grow up there will be other voices that your children will be listening to who will have some influence in their life. **One significant thing a parent can do is to identify those individuals that my children admire or who become an additional authority in their lives to engage with them and invite them into your circle.** To validate the point, who is someone outside of your immediate family that had a positive influence on you. Was it a coach or a teacher? Another family member or outside mentor? When you look back on your life and think about those people, how did they influence you and what was it that they taught you?

I remember three men in particular from my childhood and adolescence. One was Lynn Rogers, my 6th grade teacher and little league coach, who taught me about leadership and responsibility. Another was Jake Miranda, my junior high small group leader from my church. Jake taught me how to surf. He wasn't just that cool guy that the kids looked up to; he was always available for us, while also having an admirable relationship with his wife as a young married couple (they're still married to this day). The last is Jim Rhodes, who was a mentor in high school and gave me my first real job where I learned about the importance of paying attention to details and the significance of putting people first.

As you consider who was present in your life or identified the relational holes you may have had, apply this lens to the relationships in your life now. Identify some people in your circle – friends, extended family, people who already have some influence in your children's lives - and invite them to make an investment in your child's life. Being intentional about the people who have influence in your child's life will produce lifelong dividends as they are equipped with relationships and skills that will prepare them for success in life.

UNLOCKING YOUR CHILD'S POTENTIAL

One of our family's daily rituals was to quote a specific verse from the book of Proverbs. It says,

> *"For wisdom will enter your heart".*
> *(That's a really good description of courage).*
> *Knowledge will be pleasant to your soul.*
> *Discretion will protect you, and understanding will guard you.*[30]

Lets break these verses down. The first part talks about wisdom (what to do) and knowledge (how to do something). Wisdom and knowledge are

---

[30] Proverbs 2:10-11 (NIV)

connected to experiential intelligence and they produce contentment. When kids are not bound by ignorance or trapped by arrogance, they cultivate a healthy self-image. There's also discretion and understanding, the traits of emotional intelligence, that will protect and guard them. With discretion and understanding, your kids will have the emotional intelligence to know who to give their heart to and how to invest their energy and passions. In the same context, experiential intelligence equips them with a set of skills and experiences to draw from, which limits mistakes and protects them. **Developing competency is a key way to unlock your child's potential and prepares them with the skills and tools necessary for a fulfilling life.**

REFLECTION

Questions ★ ★ ★

1 What are three essential life skills that you learned from your father (or another mentor figure) that have helped you in adulthood? What are three life skills you wish someone had taught you earlier?

2 *Affection*: How often do you express affection (physically or verbally) to your child? What is one way you can be more intentional in showing them love?

3 *Observation:* Your children are watching you—what emotional reactions do they see from you most often? Are they learning healthy emotional responses from your example?

4 *Conversation:* How often do you ask your child open-ended questions about their emotions, experiences, and thoughts? How can you create more space for these conversations?

HOME
WORK

1 Write down practical skills (e.g., managing money, cooking, car maintenance) and five personal skills (e.g., decision-making, empathy, conflict resolution) that you want to teach your child that are age and stage appropriate.

PRACTICAL

PERSONAL

2 Who in your child's life (including immediate family and others) is already a **positive influence**? How can you encourage that relationship? Are there **mentors, teachers, or coaches** you could introduce to your child to expand their learning and character development? Make a list of people and look for opportunities for them to engage with your child.

After a routine colonoscopy, my wife received a stage 3 cancer diagnosis.

I grew up in a Christian home with wonderful parents and two younger brothers. My mom and dad loved the Lord and showed us how to follow Him with all our hearts. In 1993, I married the love of my life, who came from a family with nearly identical faith values. **When we started our own family, we worked hard to blend the best of both backgrounds, creating a culture that would raise strong, faith-filled children.**

Last year, my family and I faced the most challenging season of our lives. After a routine colonoscopy in March, my wife received a stage 3 cancer diagnosis. Sitting in the hospital bed, she looked at me and said with determination, "I don't have time for this!" That unwavering resilience is one of the many qualities that made me fall in love with her over thirty years ago.

After processing the shock, we called our three adult children and their spouses. **In that moment, everything we had worked for as parents came into focus.** Dad Academy's lesson on creating a healthy family culture had been a guiding principle in our home, teaching us the importance of raising confident kids who know how to lead and serve well.

My wife always emphasized deep conversations, constantly asking our kids "why" questions to help them process life intentionally. Not because she was a helicopter parent, but because we wanted our children to grow into thoughtful, strong individuals. Our kids always heard me say, "The only person you follow is Jesus. Everyone else, you lead."

So it was no surprise when, during that family call with our children and their spouses, our son immediately suggested something that would carry us through the next nine months. He proposed we have a nightly family prayer and communion until my wife was cancer-free. **And that's exactly what we did. Every single night. Through every hospital visit, chemotherapy session, and radiation treatment.** Through every uncertainty, every small victory, and even the miraculous moments that left doctors without explanations. Those calls became the lifeline that carried us through 2024, making us stronger and closer than ever before. And just in case you're wondering—the doctors confirmed what we as a family contended for on that very first night of prayer: my wife is cancer-free.

Creating a healthy family culture that produces confident kids is hard work, but it is worth every effort. In the end, we all want our children—and now our grandchildren—to do better than us, be better than us, achieve more than us, and be part of something bigger than us. If we do the work, the legacy we build will last for generations. And let me tell you, it's worth it.

Instilling Confidence

Producing a Healthy Family Culture

"

How a man is
remembered
by his children
is the true measure
of his life.

ANONYMOUS

INSTILLING CONFIDENCE

Producing a Healthy Family Culture

*J*ack dedicated his life to helping young men become men. As a head football coach, he committed himself not just to the Xs and Os, but to teaching young men the skills they would need to be successful on the field. He also understood that winning didn't just come from courage, or competence, but confidence as well, a winning attitude that was shared by every person on the team. He was committed to faith and family, and those priorities spilled over into his profession.

Through the ups and down, Jack knew the most important people he would "coach" were his own children. So they responded to every special moment in their lives the same way they addressed adversity. Jack would ask his children, "Who's got it better than us?" His children would reply "Nooooobody!"

This mantra came to define the Harbaugh family and is pointed to by NFL Super Bowl head coaches and brothers Jim and John, and sister Joani (married to NCAA Men's Basketball coach Tom Crean) for the infectious optimism that shapes their professional careers and family cultures. "Who's got it better than us? Nooooooobody!"

Unless we make a plan to be intentional fathers, we face the possibility of not being successful in the most important job in our lives. Our job as fathers is to cultivate courage, construct competency, and create confidence. Courage is related to

> **Confidence is the result of knowing who you are and what you stand for.**

the issue of developing character. Competency is about having the necessary intelligence to be able to navigate life successfully. Confidence is the result of knowing who you are and what you stand for.

THREE LEVELS OF FATHERHOOD

There are three levels to fathering. There is level one - biological. Your significant contribution to the parenting relationship is having been the sperm donor. While there are many reasons that may have contributed to the situation, there's no real sense of responsibility or obligation to the relationship with the mother or the child.

The second level is material, the provider. You do your best to make sure your family has what they need. While it may not have much personal fulfillment, there is a sense that we are doing our best to make sure the needs we are aware of are being met.

The third and highest level of fatherhood is cultural. Cultural fathering is intentionally creating an environment where courage, competency, and confidence is cultivated. This approach to fatherhood is intentional because it begins with the end goal of parting in mind. But before we can focus on what our goals for our children are, we may want to begin by asking ourselves what our goals for our own lives are. **I think we begin by asking ourselves how do you want to be remembered?**

Your Turn

_____

_____

_____

 How you want to be remembered is not about the big things that we accomplish, but it's about your presence. It's about your being. It's about what you have deposited in someone's life to help them not only become successful, but also to affirm their value and worth. This is why cultural fathering is so important.

CULTURE CREATING

Cultural fathering is focused on the culture you create in your family. Simply, culture is what distinguishes one group from another. It's the combination of attitudes which are based on our values that direct our actions. Those actions are based on our choices which are based in our belief system and structure.

We understand how culture works, ethnically, even generationally. But how does it work in families? Do families have a culture? Absolutely! **Remember culture is created by attitudes, actions and values.** It's how a family thinks, how a family feels, what it believes, why it believes, and how it acts. **Your family already has a culture. The question is, did you design it,** *or is it by default?*

Let's take a look at the three parts of the family culture. First of all, there are **CHOICES**. Choices define a family culture because it says we do this and we don't do that. It's based on the idea that every decision is actually two decisions. The decision to do one thing is also a decision not to do something else. Decisions are determined on what we do or don't do based on our commitment to a higher value. This decision framework contributes to developing courage, to living with heart, to the core of who we are, because our character is shaped by our values.

Then there are what we would call cultural **NORMS**. These are the unspoken rules that people conform or adhere to. It's the unspoken understanding of what is expected of us. This is related to being able to "read the room" and know what behavior is appropriate. For example, shaking hands and looking

COMPONENTS OF CULTURE

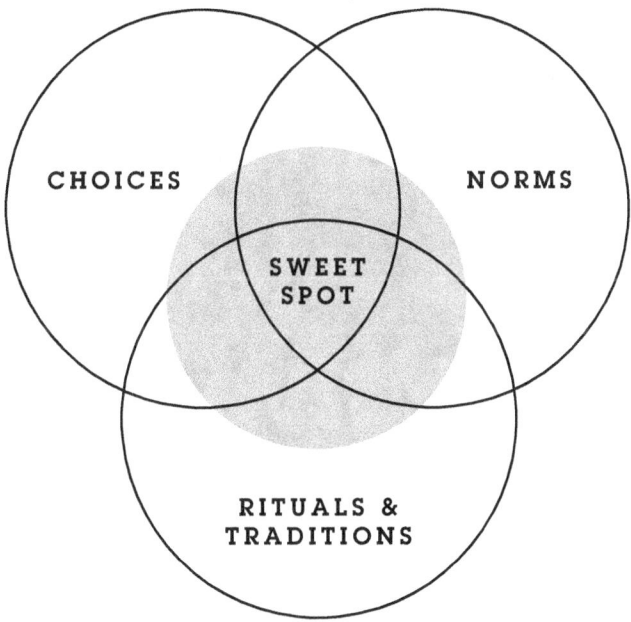

CHOICES

NORMS

SWEET SPOT

RITUALS & TRADITIONS

people in the eye is a norm for most of us in our western culture. Having coached athletes from other countries, looking a coach in the eye is considered to be disrespectful, so keeping one's head bowed when being spoken to is their cultural norm. Family norms may be words or "tone of voice" we use or don't use in our home. They may be as simple as daily expectations like making one's bed every day or clearing the table after meals. Norms are related to someone's intelligence and the development of their competency, knowing how to apply the right things in the right situations.

The third part that defines culture is the culture's **RITUALS AND TRADITIONS**.

The attention and intention you give to your family determines how you're going to be remembered.

This is what gives a family a sense of identity and security. These daily behaviors and memorable moments are what bring intention and purpose to developing one's identity and sense of security.

THE SWEET SPOT

Where your choices, norms, rituals, and traditions overlap, that's the sweet spot of purposeful parenting. It's there that your values are most visible and family life is most impactful. The sweet spots in your family life don't occur by accident. Creating

> Creating a life that your kids will remember is going to take work.

a life that your kids will remember is going to take work. As a father, the work you put into your family determines how you're going to be remembered.

There's a scripture that reminds us how we will be remembered that says this, *"We remember… your work that comes from faith, your effort that comes from love, and your perseverance that comes from hope"*.[31] We "work" at being a dad, because we have faith in what it will produce. We give our best "effort" because it is the way we demonstrate our love and our commitment to our family. And we persevere. We keep at it because there's a promise that we're working towards: developing courageous, competent, and confident kids.

---

[31] 1 Thessalonians 1:3 (NIV)

145

THE POWER OF RITUALS

If we want confident kids, we must introduce rituals and traditions into our family that define our culture. I define *rituals as the purpose-full habits and routines.* These are repeated actions that have meaning behind them.

Traditions are purpose-full events that are repeated. These are the experiences that create memories. Traditions, when combined with rituals, create patterns and bring rhythm to our lives.

> **Rituals are the purpose-full habits and routines. Traditions are purpose-full events.**

Let's talk about the daily routines and rituals of our lives. What is your daily routine? The alarm goes off, you roll out of bed and you do what? For me, it's to go to the bathroom, grab a cup of coffee, and sit down in my chair. I try to do my Bible reading first. Then I read the news, followed by a conversation with my spouse. That's how I start the day. That's a routine, my morning ritual, and my whole family knows what Dad's morning looks like.

What's important about these rituals is that, because they're repeated so often, they create a lasting image that shape how you're going to be remembered. Your kids are going to remember these rituals. I hope my kids remember seeing me reading the Scripture most days, because I value cultivating my spiritual life and the integrity it gives to my life. But I hope they'll also remember me reading to them and praying with them as they went to bed each night.

Bedtime and morning are great for rituals. Before my children left for school, we had a ritual that included quoting the same Bible verse (Proverbs 2:10-11) and a simple prayer: *"Dear Heavenly Father, let everything I say and everything I do honor You."* I've taken that prayer and brought that into my role as a high school basketball coach. Our team says this prayer every day at the end of practice. This ritual serves as a reminder of the kind of men we want to be, what we are really committed to as a team, on and off the court. This ritual helps to define our culture.

One of the simple rituals I learned that you might adopt is that I, Dad, sign the birthday cards. It's a simple action that communicates to my kids that the sentiment and celebration doesn't just come from mom, but it comes from dad too. There's also the ritual of not leaving your house without taking one of your kids with you. They may roll their eyes and even resist it, but those are the things that they'll remember. Those moments create opportunities for conversation that wouldn't exist otherwise.

In fact, I want to encourage you to develop a ritual around church or your spiritual community, because it's the one place where we are reminded that life is not about me; it's about something much bigger. When you prioritize your family schedule around some non-negotiables it puts legs to your values. Like the story of the Harbaughs at the start of the chapter, my parents had a motto for our family. I was raised with a brother that's only eighteen months younger than me. When we were little, my dad used to grab my brother and I used to tell us all the time, "Listen, brothers stick together." When our sister was added to the mix, Mom would remind us all, "family sticks together." That statement communicated the family values of

> **Rituals remind us what is important and who we are as a family.**

loyalty, commitment, sacrifice, as well as an expectation of what would be a life priority. That motto not only remains a value for my brother and sister and I, but it is now applied to our own families. As a result, our children share that value not only for each other but for the extended family as well.

These rituals are how our values are expressed, and the rituals build security because it becomes something that they can depend on. They become a way to remind us what's important and who we are as a family.

THE PURPOSE OF TRADITIONS

The partner to family rituals are our *family traditions*. When one thinks of traditions, we often go to the activities surrounding the holidays. Holidays are a built-in time to give meaning to our family's culture. Personally, part of our family holiday of traditions includes our participating in the services of our faith community. For example, we go to a worship service the night before Thanksgiving Day, because giving thanks to God is the purpose of the holiday. With very few exceptions, we've always gone to church on Christmas Eve to remember the birth of Christ. It's a way that we remember the greatest gift we have received before we go and open the gifts we have for each other. These "holy" days, and other holidays (Fourth of July and Labor Day in the US for example) provide the opportunity to repeat certain activities and create memories as a family. This just touches the surface of the power of tradition in a family's culture.

THE SIGNIFICANCE OF CELEBRATIONS

A great question to consider is **how can you build meaning into the events that are already on your calendar?** *Traditions* happen in two forms: celebrations and recreations. Let's talk about celebrations. There are birthdays and anniversaries that occur every year. How do you as a dad participate in your kids' birthday celebrations? Do you just kind of run all the errands and mom does all the rest of the work? Or do you contribute to the event in a way that adds significance and value to it? There will also be awards ceremonies or other special recognitions that will take place. Do you prioritize being present for these occasions? **Dad's participation turns a special moment into a memorable one.**

Confident kids come from healthy family cultures.

There are also everyday celebrations that you can create. I have a friend who gets up and makes blueberry pancakes for his family every Saturday. Even though his children are now young adults, they look forward to sitting around the table together having pancakes. He says he can't wait to do this with his grandkids one day. The pancakes are just a tool to create connections and make memories together. That's what dad does.

I love that my dad used to go on dates with my sister, and, as a result, I tried to do that with my daughter. She's still one of my favorite people to spend time with! Our family also likes family movie nights. I don't know what your thing is, but whatever it is, plan and make it happen! It communicates to your family that you're thinking about them, and that they are so important to you that they are worth time on your schedule.

THE IMPORTANCE OF RE-CREATION

Another part of tradition is recreation. If you break the word down it is re-creation. These are the times together that shape your family through creating experiences that form core memories. Ask yourself, **what are the things our family does and do they bring life to our family?** Many families settle for being busy, but are not intentional about the activities and experiences that shape their family. So many families' calendars revolve around their kids' activities. Simply being busy at the ball field every week or at some type of educational experience is an inadequate substitute for quality family time. I'd like to challenge you to develop an intentional thing - a shared interest or hobby that your family does together that says this is who we are.

As you reflect on the ideas of tradition and recreation, I want to encourage you as you consider how important vacations are. Creating space to rest and recalibrate is so important that it is in the top three of the Ten Commandments. Our lives run at such a busy pace that it is paramount to take a break in our lives to breathe; to make time for new experiences, make

Vacations with your family should make time and make space, not just fill time and space.

time for rest, make time for pleasure. Every family needs an extended period of time outside of their everyday life to rest and to share experiences together. That is really what the word vacation means. "Vacate" means to leave and to give up. What's so funny is that with vacations, we tend to fill it with so much busyness. The running joke is that we often need a vacation after our vacation.

Vacations with your family should make time and make space, not just fill time and space. I've discovered that with vacations, it's often the journey that is the most memorable thing, not the destination. When I think about the vacations that I grew up with, and the vacations that are most memorable with my children, it's never about the location or destination. It was always about how we got there and all the things that happened on the journey.

Rituals, these purposeful habits in our life, create security. Traditions, purposeful events create identity. Combined together they tell you who you are. All throughout the Scripture, God gave His people things to do and places to be for one purpose, so that they would remember who they are. It's an opportunity for them to tell their story and reinforce their identity. Because **when a person knows who they are and is secure in who they are, they have confidence.**

Confident kids come from healthy family cultures. Dad, you are the culture creator and therefore the memory maker. You have a family culture. Is it one you've designed with intention or defaulted to? It's never too late to start creating your family culture. Consider the kind of rituals you're going to develop daily, weekly, monthly that build into your children a sense of value and security. What kind of traditions are you going to build into your family's calendar? How can you bring extra meaning into your holidays and the personal traditions you create that will produce a healthy identity? This is important work because this is what a dad will be remembered for.

REFLECTION
Questions ★ ★ ★

1 Are you primarily operating at the **biological, material, or cultural** level of fatherhood? What steps can you take to move toward **cultural fathering**—intentionally shaping your family's identity and values?

2 How would you describe the **culture of your family**? Is it intentional or by default? Do you feel like your family culture has found its sweet spot?

3 What **daily, weekly, or seasonal rituals** does your family already practice? Do they reinforce your values?

4 Think about a **tradition** from your childhood that had a lasting impact on you. How can you introduce or adapt something similar for your own family?

HOME
WORK

(1) Choose one new daily or weekly ritual that strengthens your family connection (e.g., morning check-ins, bedtime routines, gratitude moments, or family dinners).

MY NEW RITUAL

---

(2) Identify upcoming events (**birthday, holiday, or special occasion**) and brainstorm ways to **add extra meaning** to the event's traditions. Plan the event so that it aligns with your family values and strengthens bonds.

EVENTS

EXTRA MEANING

(3) Plan a family **vacation or getaway**—big or small—that allows for **rest and connection**, rather than just filling the time with activities.

DATE

LOCATION

BUDGET

_____

_____

_____

PLANS FOR CONNECTION

_____

_____

_____

(4) How do you want your children to remember you? Write the vision down. What specific actions are you taking today that contribute to that legacy?

_____

_____

_____

_____

Chris

I realized then that sacrifices are necessary to give my children the time and presence I never had.

I grew up in a single-parent household where my mother raised four sons alone. My father's addiction kept him from being present, and though he longed for a relationship with us, his choices created a divide. On his deathbed, he desperately wanted to speak to us, but tubes down his throat made it impossible. That moment left an indelible mark on me—I realized then that sacrifices are necessary to give my children the time and presence I never had. I vowed to be a present father because I saw firsthand how the absence of those conversations and teachings shaped my journey into adulthood.

As a father, I've faced many struggles and obstacles. **One of the biggest challenges has been modeling what love and a healthy family dynamic should look like in our home.** Neither my wife nor I had a consistent example of that growing up. We had to learn how to build a strong marriage, how to communicate effectively, and how to put in the effort to make it work. Another major obstacle has been choosing time over money. There were financial opportunities I could have pursued, but they would have taken me away from my family for long periods. Instead, we made the decision to create a business that allows us to move as a unit. Everything we do, we do together.

That decision has been the most rewarding of my life, allowing me to be fully engaged, supportive, and present as a father.

Through my experience with Dad Academy, I**'ve learned the importance of consistency—being the same leader, mentor, and teacher at home that I am at work. I used to see those as separate roles, but now I understand they are one and the same.** Dad Academy encouraged me to be intentional in balancing these roles to meet the unique needs of my children. One of the most valuable lessons I've learned is that each of my children requires a different version of Dad to thrive. Their learning styles, personalities, and emotional needs vary, and I have to adapt my approach to truly connect with each of them.

This awareness has shaped my parenting style, making me more patient, present, and proactive in providing the guidance and support my kids need. **I now approach fatherhood with greater intention, knowing that my presence, adaptability, and love will help them grow into the best versions of themselves.**

CHAPTER

Making Life Memorable

Milestone Moments and Significant Ceremonies

"

Children are not
a distraction from
more important work.
They are the most
important work.

C.S. LEWIS

MAKING LIFE MEMORABLE

Milestone Moments and Significant Ceremonies

*D*o you remember your child's first steps? There's a lot of steps between those first steps and the steps they'll take to receive their high school diploma, or the walk down the aisle to become a spouse. It's said that as a parent, the days are long but the years are short. As a father whose children are now grown, I can tell you the time you spend journeying with your children is both challenging and rewarding. It is also over far more quickly than we anticipate. **That's why it's so important for a Dad to have a map of sorts that will guide him and his journey's with his family.** Let's take a second to review the journey we've been on in Dad Academy and the steps that we've been taking to being a purposeful parent.

STEPS ON THE PARENTING PATH

The first step in purposeful parenting is understanding our center, the values that we live by. We learn that fatherhood is not about doing everything right, it's about doing the right things. In step two we begin to learn that really being a dad is about sacrifice. In order for dad to give life to something, he has to be willing to lose his. Step three has to do about choices; that a dad's choices reflect his thinking. In the Bible there's a verse that says *as a man thinks in his heart, so is he.* [32] This reminds us that our values determine our choices which direct our life's decisions and ultimately determine our legacy. The fourth step is about training. The *training* we give our kids, and being trustworthy as a father, produces courage in their lives. Step five in being an intentional father is understanding that *intelligence* produces competence, which unlocks your child's potential. The next step,

> **The time you spend journeying with your children is both challenging and rewarding. It is also over far more quickly than we anticipate.**

step six, is where our intention becomes practical and repeatable. We create daily *rituals*, the purposeful habits that create security, and build family *traditions*, the purposeful events that create identity. It's identity and security that creates confidence in the life of our kids. Now, you're starting to begin to formulate a plan.

You begin to understand your mission as a dad to create courage, to develop competence, and cultivate confidence in your kids. You do this through

30 Proverbs 2:10-11 (NIV)

discipline (training), intelligence (wisdom), and creating your family's culture. You know where you parent from (values) and what your goal is. You know what you're going to pass on to your kids and where you actually need to ask other people for help. You're going to develop better dad habits and make time for your family, not just fill time and establish significant traditions. All because we've learned how a man is remembered by his children is the true measure of a man. So, how do we know how we're doing? How can we measure our success?

MILESTONE MOMENTS

Let me suggest that one significant way is by creating milestone events and using the power of ceremony. What are some ceremonies in our culture? Weddings, graduations, bar mitzvahs, and getting driver's licenses are all events that signify a life change. **I want you to look back over your life and think about what was a milestone memory in your life? Why was it significant? What happened? Who was there and what was it about?**

Your Turn

What we learn from analyzing these memorable moments in our life, is that each one of these ceremonies really marks the end of one season and the start of another. These kinds of ceremonies are embedded into certain cultures. For example, in the Jewish culture, there's the *Bar/Bat Mitzvah*. Bar means son, Bat means daughter, and *Mitzvah* means "commandment" or "good deed." At thirteen years old for boys, twelve for girls, the ceremony signifies that they have become a son or daughter of "good deeds", connected to their immediate community and history as a people. It also says that they are now accountable for their actions and are invited to participate in the community as an adult.

> **Ceremonies mark new seasons that come with new privileges and new responsibilities.**

For young ladies in certain Latino cultures, there's the *Quinceanera*. This coming-of-age ceremony celebrates a young woman of fifteen years old, introducing her to her community and acknowledging that she has moved from childhood into womanhood. She has a set of skills and a certain level of capacity that now she is recognized as being prepared for marriage and the responsibility of taking care of a family.

One of the challenges in our western culture is that we don't have very

many ceremonies that help people know when they move from one stage to another. Yet, they are very important because they signal a transition, a new season that is embedded with new privileges and new responsibilities. Ceremonies are also powerful because they help us remember, both what we were and who we are becoming. Lastly, ceremonies are helpful for Dad because they affirm our trust in our children, celebrate steps towards success, and reinforce our family's culture.

FOUR SEASONS FOR SIGNIFICANT CEREMONIES

You may have heard the term "rites of passage." It describes these significant ceremonies or memorable moments that will help you communicate to your children when they have moved from one stage to another. I think that there are four seasons for ceremonies in the life of our child.

The first one is from when they go from *child to teen*, kind of in the puberty age, 12 - 16 years old. When my son turned twelve, we celebrated his birthday by going out to breakfast. There I laid out for him our plan for the next twelve months. Once a month, we would go have breakfast and talk about the qualities of being a man. Then we would go out for "training" where I passed on skills I had. For example, one Saturday we built something using my power tools. Another weekend I taught him how to do his laundry, iron clothes, and shine shoes. The final weekend, he had to plan a date with his Mom, including making a dinner reservation, opening doors for her, and paying the bill (with

As a parent, the days may be long but the years are short.

the cash I had given him).

The conclusion of what we called "The Year of The Man" was a ceremony at his thirteenth birthday where all the men in his biological family, uncles and grandfathers, gave him a letter on the qualities of manhood we had been studying, and we prayed a blessing over him. My daughter experienced something similar from my wife and myself the year before she turned sixteen, which culminated in a special trip to New York City and her own special ceremony, similar in format to her brother's, but uniquely designed for her.

The second season or transition from one life stage to another is when they move from *teen to adulthood*. For example, a natural transition for this stage is high school graduation. While the graduation ceremony is already an important one, we wanted to add value to it by giving them significant, personal, and thoughtful gifts that helped to keep a God-sized vision of their future in front of them and a reminder of the people who were there to support them.

There's also another transition that happens when they move from what I'm going to call from *student to skilled*. This could be when they move beyond your house and into developing their own life, in their own career, and they begin to take personal responsibility fully for their life. Even the mundane tasks of buying household items such as bedding and kitchenware can be a memorable moment when the event is marked by significance and communicates value.

The final season that's worth acknowledging is when they move from a *single life to a shared life*, when they take responsibility for the love and well-being of another person in marriage. It was a joy at our son's wedding rehearsal dinner for him to receive gifts from the men in our family that symbolized what he would need as a husband.

When we intentionally recognize these stages of life with ceremony and create memorable moments, we help them understand that they've moved forward in their life and communicate their value and worth.

FOUR ELEMENTS FOR CREATING MEMORABLE MOMENTS

There are also four elements to every significant ceremony. The first and most important thing is that the ceremony should communicate the celebrant's *value*. An effective ceremony says to the celebrant that they are important and this moment is important! Therefore, consideration should be given to how the ceremony communicates worth and significance to the celebrant.

Secondly, because we want to communicate a sense of value, making our child feel important in this moment, memorable moments also use *symbols*. Just like a wedding uses a ring or graduation gives a diploma, a significant ceremony should have some sort of symbol to mark the occasion. The importance of the symbol(s) is not ascribed by the cost of an item but in what it represents to the giver and communicates to the recipient.

As mentioned earlier, for my daughter's sixteenth birthday, we sent her on a trip to New York City with her mom for a girls' weekend, doing many of the things she loved. Upon arriving home, I had a special gift for her: a set of pearls that belonged to her maternal grandmother. This gift would remind her of the elegance with which she's invited to live, and that no matter the status of her life, these pearls remind her that she has value.

Pearls also have symbolic significance. They form when an irritant like a grain of sand gets inside of the mollusk. When the irritant becomes covered in a secretion that builds up over time, a shell that encases the grain of sand. The pearl is a reminder that something beautiful can come from something painful. Additionally, the string of pearls reminds her that she comes from a long line of women who were beautiful, both inside and out.

These symbols should also represent a *vision*. The memorable moment should inform and inspire the celebrant with a vision (describing what's ahead), a code of conduct (for the new privileges and responsibilities), a cause (defining the benefit and cost of growth, development and sacrifice), and a blessing (offering your personal and their community's support). Our privilege and responsibility as a father is to help our children develop a vision, a dream, for what each new season holds and what life could be like if they're willing to give the attention and effort to make it a reality.

The final consideration is the *cost* of the ceremony. Now, cost is more than financial, but it has to do with the time and the effort and the thought that you've put into this, making this a meaningful moment in their life. The more time, thought, planning, effort, and money invested towards the celebration, the more memorable it will be. Planning should be in proportion to the significance of the event. This will help to determine the amount of time and energy to be invested along with financial considerations. Significant ceremonies can be as simple as a single activity (like a party), or as detailed as a multi-day experience (like a special trip) or an intentional process (the accomplishment of a task or project).

Ceremonies affirm significance. That's why it's so important for you to make a plan to acknowledge these milestone moments, create memories, and use the power of ceremony to celebrate the growth and development of your kids as they move from stage to stage.

THE THREE RESPONSIBILITIES OF A FATHER

The responsibilities of being a father are more than just what you are able to provide financially or support emotionally. Research proves the importance of a father's presence in a child's life. Beyond being present, a purposeful father is intentional with fulfilling his responsibilities. Your child's well-being is dependent upon your attention to these three dimensions of their lives.

> **The responsibilities of being a father are more than just what you are able to provide financially or support emotionally.**

Protect their purity. Kids grow up so quickly. You can't stop them from growing up, but you can make sure that it happens at a reasonable pace. To do so, you have to spend time with them to be able to understand where they are in their emotional development, their physical development, and their sexual development. **And we want to make sure that we allow their hearts and their souls to be unpolluted by any other message other than their value and their worth.** While we can't prevent that natural process of growing up from happening, it's our job to make sure that it happens at a pace that is appropriate for whatever stage of life they are in.

Affirm their identity. At some point, kids become self-conscious. They start comparing themselves to others, and that becomes a threat to their self-confidence. **Part of our job as fathers is to not let their self-worth and value be defined or influenced by an image of what others want them to be.** Through the years they may try on different personas and different trends that change with every season or new friend group. But our responsibility is to be

Values determine our choices which direct our life's decisions and ultimately determine our legacy.

unchanging in the way we embrace them, affirm them, and remind them of their worth and value.

Direct them to their destiny. I hope you believe that there is inherent greatness in your child. Your role is not to extract it out of them, but to nurture it within them. The most powerful way to do this is to teach them the value of service. Our culture generally trains people in the ways of consumerism—where satisfying my feelings, my cravings, and my needs is what gives my life value. The greatest thing a dad models for his children is that life has most meaning when life is not about you, but when you are giving your life away for the greater good and for the good of those around you.

REFLECTION
Questions ★ ★ ★

1 Think back to a milestone moment in your own life. What made it significant? Who was involved? How did it shape you?

2 What are some milestone moments you have already celebrated with your child? Were they meaningful? How could they have been more intentional?

 **3** How could recognizing and celebrating milestones help your child feel seen, valued, and prepared for the next stage of life?

 **4** How are you **guiding your child toward their destiny**? What opportunities are you providing to help them develop a **purpose beyond themselves?**

HOME WORK

1 Identify your child's current life stage and the next major transition they will experience (e.g., moving from childhood to adolescence, graduating, leaving home).

2 If you don't already have a structured way of celebrating major life transitions, create one (e.g., a special trip, a dinner with family elders, a letter-writing tradition). Commit to repeating this ritual for each of your children as they reach the same stage

MOMENT   CELEBRATE

_____   _____

MOMENT   CELEBRATE

_____   _____

MOMENT   CELEBRATE

_____   _____

MOMENT   CELEBRATE

_____   _____

MOMENT   CELEBRATE

_____   _____

(3) Choose one **upcoming milestone moment*** and write out the following:

MOMENT

_____

WHAT THE MILESTONE REPRESENTS

_____

HOW YOU WILL AFFIRM YOUR CHILD'S GROWTH

_____

_____

_____

A MEANINGFUL SYMBOL OR GIFT TO REINFORCE THE OCCASION

_____

* Visit DadAcademy.info to download the Milestone Moment Planner for a step-by-step guide to planning a rite of passage

A VISION OR BLESSING TO SHARE DURING THE CEREMONY

Gordy

Losing my dad when I was 25 left a void. There were so many moments when I wish I had someone to turn to for advice.

I was fortunate to have had a close relationship with my father. Unfortunately, that relationship ended too soon due to his battle with cancer. The lessons he taught me have profoundly shaped the father, husband, and person I am today. I am forever grateful for the values he instilled in me—having a strong moral compass, being selfless, and maintaining a positive attitude.

My dad was a man of principle. He had an unwavering sense of right and wrong—there was no middle ground. He also had a generous heart, always valuing others and leading with kindness. There was never a doubt in my mind about how much he cared for me and those around him. At the same time, he had high expectations. He made it clear that a good attitude and maximum effort were non-negotiable. Looking back, I see how much those expectations shaped me.

As a father of four, one of my biggest challenges has been balancing my time and resources on the "right" things. Life is full of distractions, and every year it seems like there are more. To keep myself focused, I constantly ask two questions: 1. How will I measure my life and success? 2. Who will be sitting next to me in my rocking chair when I'm older? Having answers to these questions helps me prioritize what truly matters.

Losing my dad at twenty-five meant that I haven't had a father figure in my adult life. That has been a struggle, especially as a young father myself. There are so many moments when I wish I had someone to turn to for advice—someone I could trust, who had been through it all before.

Dad Academy gave me the structure and motivation to be more intentional in my approach to fatherhood. **It's easy to dream about the kind of father you want to be; the hard part is executing that vision.** Creating my Dad Plan helped me develop a concrete action plan and hold myself accountable. More than anything, it reminded me of the incredible impact I can have on my kids. **God has given me the blessing of being a father, and I want to make the most of it.**

CHAPTER

The Dad Plan™

Planning is bringing the future into the present so you can do something about it now.

ALAN LAKEIN

THE DAD PLAN™

*T*here are approximately 936 weeks between your child's birth and their 18th birthday. I know that seems like a lot. Here's another number: 52. Fifty-two is the number of weeks you'll spend with your children from their 18th birthday to the end of their father's life. The bridge between the two timelines is the fact that the more intentional a father is, the more influential he will be. Your influence comes from your presence. Your impact will come from your purpose…leading your family for good!

PLAN YOUR WORK & WORK YOUR PLAN

Men feel most successful when they know what is expected of them and have a plan to accomplish it. If a man is headed to the gym, he has a plan. If he has a financial goal, he has a plan. The challenge with being a father is that it's the only thing a man does in his life without a plan. **Because of the pace of life, fathers are, at best, responsive to situations and opportunities in their children's lives. At worst, we are reactive, having our decisions dictated by the demands on our time and resources (including emotional resources).**

What if we were able to transform our desire to be a good dad into actual actionable items? That's why every man needs a personalized DadPlan™.

Your Turn

_____

_____

_____

There is a popular adage often attributed to Benjamin Franklin, the father of time management, "Failing to plan is planning to fail." No man wants to be a failure at being a father. It would be a worthy investment of your time to develop a plan for being an intentional father. Planning involves more than setting goals; it's about creating a roadmap for success. This strategic approach to parenting offers four powerful benefits for you and your family:

Focus and Clarity

A father's job is to pass on his values and skills to his children. Establishing a clear plan helps identify family priorities and outlines the necessary steps to achieve desired outcomes, minimizing distractions and maintaining focus on what truly matters.

Improved Decision-Making

By anticipating potential parenting scenarios and formulating strategies in advance, a well-structured plan enhances decision-making when challenges arise. This proactive approach is particularly effective in guiding children's development in alignment with family values. This approach enables fathers to thoughtfully identify when to compliment and praise his children as well as when to confront and offer constructive guidance.

Intentionality and Effectiveness

As children progress through various developmental stages, intentional parenting becomes crucial. Preparing them for life requires breaking down significant tasks into manageable, actionable steps. This approach makes it feel less overwhelming, but also

> "Failing to plan is planning to fail."
> - Benjamin Franklin

increases overall effectiveness in preparing children for future milestones.

Motivation and Accountability

Implementing a tangible plan that is integrated with your schedule fosters a sense of accomplishment and provides motivation to stick to it.. Be sure to include special family events, one-on-one time with each child, and family vacation time in your planning to create lasting memories and strengthen bonds.

By diligently working your DadPlan™, you can seize the moments that leave a lasting positive impact on your family.

GETTING STARTED

To get started, you'll need a pad of paper and your calendar. Then let's work this out step by step...

STEP 1: VALUES-DRIVEN PARENTING

If a father's mission is to pass on his values to his children, he must first define those values. The first step of creating your DadPlan™ is to discover who you are, at your core. Specifically, *you need to know your values.* As described in Chapter 1, your values are the internal beliefs you hold that shape your decision-making. We all have values. But we rarely make them explicit. Naming them helps us understand ourselves. And it helps us make decisions more intentionally–living in alignment with who we aspire to be.

On your paper (or computer software) list out some of the values that you consider important. Then list out some of the roles and relationships in your life. How do you see the values being lived out in the various areas of your life? This helps us get to the "why." The values that share the most connection points to the various parts of your life will form your core values. Try to keep the list to 3-10 words or statements that best describe what your values are.

Once your values are defined, you'll have to turn them into life choices. For example, if spiritual growth and community is a value for your family, it must shape your behavior and guide your decisions. What happens when your child's sports or club schedule conflicts with service times for your church? Whatever event is made to be the priority is truly reflective of your actual values. And without it being described, our kids will discern what is most important by which event gets the ongoing priority for our participation. Our everyday life choices train our kids in our family values. Take your list of values and see if they actually pass the priority test. If your decisions don't align with your values, then you either need to adapt your values to accurately reflect your decisions, or adjust your family's commitments to values-based choices.

> **An intentional, values-based approach to training your children will help them become the best version of themselves.**

Values also are the guide for how we train or discipline our children (see Chapter 4). Being a parent does include the challenging task of correction. But what determines the behavior that needs to be confronted and corrected? Yes, your values. Your values also serve as a powerful tool to shape your child's character as you catch them doing the right things as well. Complimenting the

The more intentional a father is, the more influential he will be.

behavior that you want repeated is a great way to reinforce your values. Take some time to make a list of the behaviors you're going to compliment and correct in your children. An intentional, values-based approach to training your children will help them become the best version of themselves.

STEP 2: PREPARE YOUR CHILDREN FOR LIFE

Whatever you know how to do, you need to pass those skills onto your children. And whatever you don't know how to do, you probably have a relationship with someone who does.

There are "hard" skills to pass down (experiential intelligence): manual skills such as using tools and fixing things, household skills such as cooking and cleaning, and practical skills such as budgeting and calendaring. There are also "soft" skills (emotional intelligence) to teach: like communication, teamwork, personal responsibility, and problem-solving. For example, when our children are small, we teach them relational skills such as saying "please" and "thank you." We train them to make eye contact with people when they are being spoken to, and not to interrupt. We also teach them life skills like tying their shoes or making their bed. This kind of training goes on throughout their childhood and adolescence.

It's important for Dads not to assume that these skills will just be learned as your children go through life. Rather, we can be intentional about creating opportunities to help our kids acquire these skills at the appropriate age or stage. You must have a plan for this kind of intentional training.

Cory, the dad profiled in Chapter 5, was unsure what skills he had to pass on or how to do it. So, he went and asked his eight-year-old, "Is there anything you wish you knew how to do?" The child's response was, "I'd like to have a bank account!" This gave the dad some rails to run on. Together they made a plan for the child to earn some money.

Once they had saved the minimum required to open a checking account, he taught them some basic budgeting; keep this much for your wants and needs, set aside this much to give to others, and save the rest for the future! Together, they went and opened a savings account, for which the son and the father were both so pleased with this accomplishment!

While the primary responsibility for our child's growth and development lies with us, we understand that there are other people - family members, coaches, teachers, mentors - who become a part of that process. As it's said, "it takes a village to raise a child." What is important is that you build a relationship with these other important people in your child's life. It's worth the time to identify the people that are already investing in your children's lives. It's also worth considering who is in your relationship circle that would be a good influence on your children. Write those names down and be intentional about creating opportunities to engage them in your family's life.

STEP 3: CREATE YOUR FAMILY CULTURE

Rituals (purpose-full habits) and traditions (purpose-full events) are the glue for your family. They reflect your values and create a sense of security and identity in our family. Go back and take a look again at Chapter 6.

Now, let's start to identify moments in our daily routines and weekly life rhythms to create connections with our children. When we have little ones, bath time and bedtime are special moments for Dad to prioritize connecting with his children. As they get older, weekly family dinners and game nights create opportunities for laughter and conversation. Maybe you put notes in lunch bags, or have a "gratitude jar."[33] Maybe you have a family slogan or prayer that's said every day. These are not new ideas.

The reality is that these kinds of engaging moments are sacrificed when they are not scheduled and prioritized. These kinds of rituals are predictable anchors in life that our children can rely on which make them feel safe and secure. Over time they reaffirm a father's priority of his family and creates trust and dependability. What are some things you can make sure become a part of your daily and weekly routine? Write them into your plan.

---

[33] Each time you feel especially grateful for something throughout the year, write it down on a piece of paper and pop it into your family gratitude jar. Then at the end of the year, spend some time reading and reflecting on all the wonderful things you felt grateful for during the year.

One of the most powerful tools in our parenting toolbox are our family's traditions. **Traditions serve as the memory catalog for a family.** Some are as simple as the menu items for Thanksgiving, or when Christmas presents are opened (Christmas Eve or Christmas morning?). Every family celebration -

holidays, birthdays, anniversaries, graduations and other achievement ceremonies - should reflect your family values and communicate the individual value of each family member.

> While you cannot stop time, you can infuse it's passing with meaning.

There are many types of traditions- weekly family dinner, family recipes to pass down from one generation to another, parent-child "dates", community service projects, annual vacations–all form a collective memory which shapes our identity. This leads us to Step 4...

STEP 4: COMMIT TO CALENDAR

Remember the quote at the beginning of the chapter? "Planning is bringing the future into the present so that you can do something about it now." The only way to guarantee that these ideas turn into action is to commit them to your calendar. How are you going to make the most of the upcoming events that are already on your calendar, birthdays, anniversaries, graduations, etc.? Then you take it to the next level by scheduling time with your kids every week or every month.

Additionally, no DadPlan™ is complete without committing time and resources towards a vacation. As we discussed in Chapter 6, it is important to "vacate," to leave the everyday routines and recalibrate. Remember, vacation should create time to connect, not fill time with activities. Don't put it off, no matter how big or small. Write these things down in your calendar and make a commitment to make sure it happens.

STEP 5: HAVE A VISION FOR THE FUTURE

Many parents who have raised their children encourage young parents to make the most of the time they have with their children because, "you blink and they grow up overnight. You wonder where the time has gone." While you cannot stop time, you can infuse its passing with meaning. Whatever stage of life your kids are in right now, there's a new one approaching quickly. That's why planning memorable moments is so important. These are the special ceremonies that will help you and your children step into new seasons of life with the confidence and affirmation that they need to know they are moving ahead in life. Look ahead a few months, even years, and start to plan these special and significant events.

DEDICATE YOUR PLAN

Now that you've taken these practical steps, it is important for you to invite

A man's greatest legacy may not be what he's accomplished, but who he's raised.

your parenting partner or spouse to share this journey with you. Some guys have scheduled a date night with their spouse and shared their DadPlan™ with them. Their wives expressed that they have never been more proud of their husbands. There are few things that give our spouses a greater sense of security than seeing that we as husbands and fathers are clear on what is really important in life.

I also think there is another important step. Can I suggest that you dedicate this plan to God? It's important for us to understand that we're not asking God to partner with us. Actually, I really believe that the plan that you've developed is about you getting on the same page with God about His dreams and desires for the lives that He's entrusted to you.

A MAN'S LEGACY

I believe that a man's greatest legacy may not be what he's accomplished, but who he's raised. I believe that because you are a father that you're a man of significance, of influence beyond your understanding, simply by being a loving and intentional father. I pray that as you give your life to this significant responsibility, that you would experience the joy of shaping your family and changing the world for good.

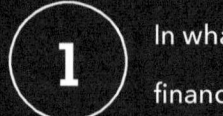

REFLECTION Questions ★ ★ ★

1 In what areas of life do you naturally create plans (fitness, career, finances, etc.)?

2 What would a "DadPlan™" look like for you? What key areas would you include?

 Think of a recent parenting challenge—how might having a plan
have helped you navigate it better?

 What are some potential parenting situations you could plan for
in advance?

 How do you want your children to remember their childhood
with you?

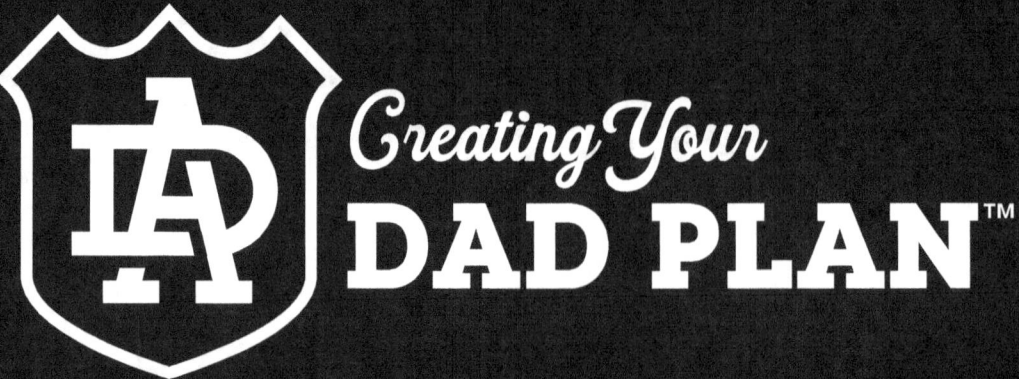

Creating Your
DAD PLAN™

Step 1
Understand What Values Are

---

(1) **List Your Values**

Narrow it down to 3-6 core values that define who you are.

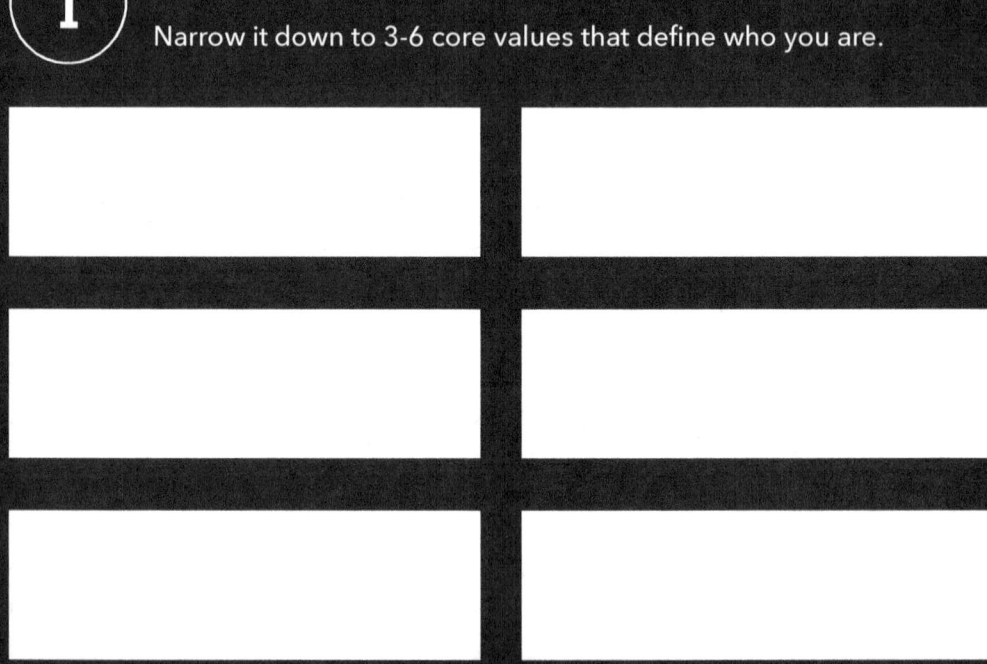

(2) Test Your Priorities

Look at your weekly schedule. Do your commitments reflect your values? Identify one change you need to make to better align your actions with your values.

_____

_____

_____

(3) Define Family Priorities

dentify how these values will guide your family's decisions about time, activities, and commitments.

_____

_____

_____

_____

(4) **Train Your Children Through Your Values**

Write down 3-4 behaviors in your children you want to compliment that reflect your values, and 3-4 behaviors that need to be watched so they can be corrected and adjusted to be aligned with your family values.

Make a plan to reinforce these behaviors by using your values as the guidelines for discipline.

Step 2
Understand What Values Are

---

(1) **Ask Your Child**

Have a conversation with your child and ask, "What's something you wish you knew how to do?" Write down their response and make a plan to teach them.

_____

_____

_____

_____

_____

_____

_____

_____

(2) **List Life Skills**

Write down a couple "hard" skills (experiential) and "soft" skills (relational) you want to teach your child that are appropriate for their current age and stage.

SOFT SKILLS   HARD SKILLS

_____   _____

_____   _____

_____   _____

_____   _____

_____   _____

(3) **Create a Teaching Plan**

Pick one skill from your list and break it into three simple steps. Schedule time to teach it to your child.

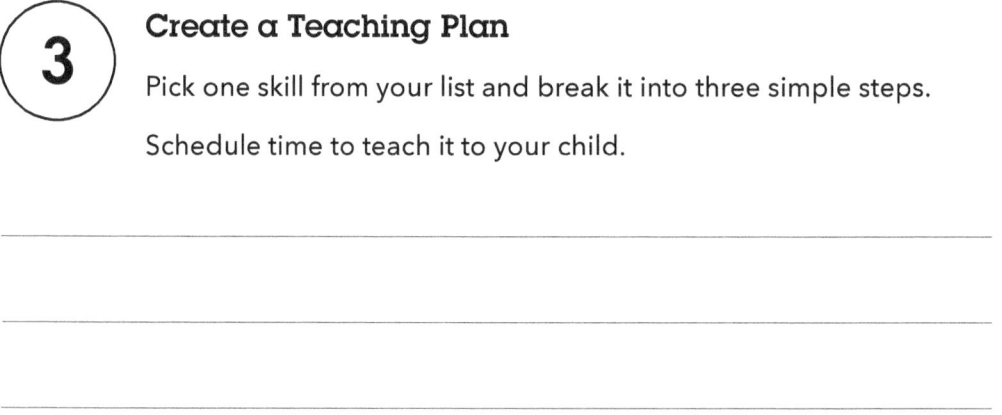

_____

_____

_____

(4) Identify Helpers

Write the names of three people in your life who have valuable skills or positive influence. Plan one way to involve them in your child's learning.

1.

2.

3.

(5) Build Learning Opportunities

Identify one way to create an intentional learning moment for each child a couple of times a year—whether it's a hands-on project, a conversation, or an experience with a mentor.child's learning.

1.

2.

3.

4.

Step 3
Create Your Family Culture

---

(1) **Identify Daily & Weekly Rituals**

List three small daily or weekly habits you can start to create connection (e.g., bedtime stories, morning check-ins, or family dinners).

1.

2.

3.

(2) **Identify Daily & Weekly Rituals**

Write down at least three traditions your family already practices (e.g., holiday customs, birthday celebrations, or seasonal activities). Identify the activities and the relationships that give these traditions significance.

1.

2.

3.

(4) **Engage Your Family**

Talk with your child(ren) about which rituals or traditions they enjoy the most. Ask for their ideas on something new to try together.

Step 4
Commit to Calendar

---

(1) **Review Your Calendar**

Look at upcoming family events (birthdays, anniversaries, graduations, etc.). Write down one way you can be intentional in making each event meaningful.

EVENT   EVENT   EVENT

_____   _____   _____

_____

_____

(2) **Schedule One-on-One Time**

Choose a specific day in the month to spend intentional time with each child. Add it to your calendar.

DATE

_____

 **Plan a Vacation**

Set a date, even if it's a simple weekend getaway or a day trip.

Write it in your calendar now. Add a vacation line item to your family budget.

DATE   LOCATION   BUDGET

_____   _____   _____

 **Prioritize Connection Over Activity**

When planning family time, focus on experiences that foster

conversation and bonding rather than just busy schedules.

 **Set a Reminder**

Use your phone or planner to set a reminder for family

commitments so they don't get lost in the busyness of life.

Step 5

Have a Vision for the Future

(1) **Reflect on Your Child's Current Stage**

Write down what stage of life your child is in now and what the next stage will be.

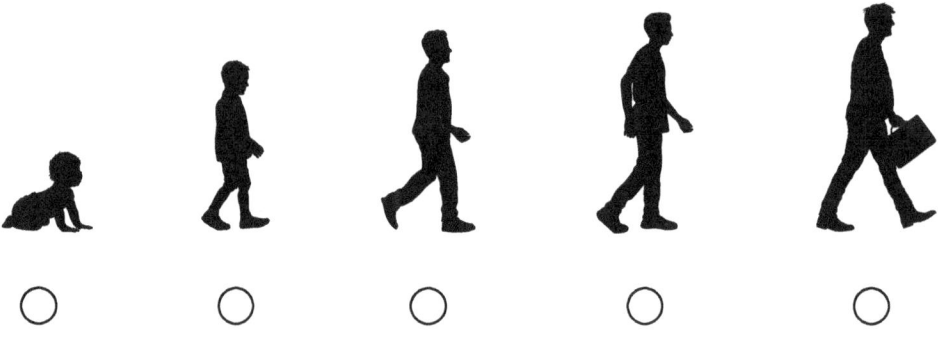

○   ○   ○   ○   ○

(2) **Identify Key Milestones**

List upcoming life transitions (starting school, becoming a teenager, graduation, first job, etc.).

_____   _____   _____

_____   _____   _____

_____   _____   _____

(3) Plan a Meaningful Ceremony

Choose a way to mark each milestone with a special event, tradition, or affirmation. Write it in your calendar.

_____ _____ _____

_____ _____ _____

_____ _____ _____

(4) Create a Long-Term Vision

Think ahead 1, 5, or 10 years. What kind of relationship do you want with your child? What kind of person do you hope they become? Write down a few intentional steps to help guide them there.

_____

_____

_____

(5) Capture the Moments

Be intentional about documenting these milestones through photos, journals, or letters to your child.

Looking back, I realize now that fatherhood isn't just about biology— it's about presence, sacrifice, and leading by example.

Fatherhood, for me, has always been about resilience, responsibility, and showing up. **My biological father left when I was three, leaving my mom to raise three kids on her own** while working as a secretary. We didn't have much, but she made sure we never felt like we were lacking—especially on birthdays and Christmas. She had a way of making things special, no matter how tight money was.

Without a father in the house, my older brother and future brother-in-law stepped in to fill the gap. They taught me discipline, hard work, and integrity, sometimes without even realizing it. And church? That wasn't optional. It was a foundational part of our lives, shaping my values and giving me a sense of direction. Looking back, I realize now that fatherhood isn't just about biology— it's about presence, sacrifice, and leading by example.

One of the biggest challenges I've faced as a father is learning that each of my children requires a different kind of parenting. Even though they grew up in the same home, under the same rules, and with the same values, their personalities and emotional needs couldn't be more different. My oldest is fiercely independent and quick to move on from conflict, while my youngest is more sensitive and needs time to process things.

Early on, I made the mistake of trying to parent them the same way. I thought if I was fair and consistent, that would be enough. It wasn't. I had to learn to adjust my approach, to meet them where they were instead of where I expected them to be. And honestly? I'm still working on that—except now, they're both married with families of their own. I have a feeling this lesson will follow me into my role as "Pops."

Going through the Dad Academy workshop was an incredible experience— not just for me, but for my two sons-in-law, who went through it with me. I've said many times that these two young men are more prepared for marriage and fatherhood than I ever was—maybe even more than I am now. If my wife and I had been given the chance to design the perfect husbands for our daughters, we couldn't have done any better.

The best part of Dad Academy, at this stage in my life, was watching them grow through it. Seeing their perspectives evolve, their commitment to being great husbands and fathers solidify—it gave me a deep sense of peace. **I know our family is in good hands, or rather, in God's hands, for generations to come.**

Ackowledgments

*I*t's often said that it takes a village to raise a child. In my case, it took a village to publish a book. I want to take a moment to thank some very special people who helped make this dream a reality.

This book was crowdfunded by an incredible community of supporters. I'm deeply grateful to those who contributed: Ken & JoAnn Lickel, Roger & Sally Biehn, Tim & Kari Carlson, Doug & Atousa Johnson, Clemente & Vanessa Bonilla, John & Liz Vallejo, Breaking the Cycle Foundation, Tim & Diane Andrews, Sean & Stephanie McDowell, Randy & Sandy Remington, Fritz & Darcy Maskrey, Luc & Ashleigh Ceci, John & CJ Rapp, David & Beth DeCubellis, Nick & Lisa Gordon, and four very special ladies who believe deeply in the mission of equipping dads: Vickie Davenport, Laura Massey, Roxie McIntosh, and Ashley Schiermeyer.

Thanks also to the Dad Academy advisory board: Ken Lickel, Fritz Maskrey, and Mike Ogburn, and to content advisors, Rick Steinberg, Kelly Fellows, and Eyal Aronoff. Over one thousand men have gone through the Dad Academy workshop.

I'm especially grateful for the ten men who shared their personal fatherhood stories in this book: Mea Wong, Nick Gordon, Brad Hamilton (my brother), Sean Hood (my nephew), Fritz Maskrey, Cory Liebrum, Tim Vercellono (my brother-in-law), Chris Childress, Gordy Stead, and Darren Cruzan. Your transparency and courage are inspiring.

A huge thank you to Bryce Reyes of Bryce Reyes Design for bringing his creative genius to the design and presentation of the book, and for his shared passion for fathers. Steve Norman was the perfect editor for me, bringing his literary and pastoral expertise to the project. I'm also grateful to Karen Campbell of Karen Campbell Media, an incredible partner who believes in the Dad Academy mission. A special thank you to Bob Hunt and Foursquare Mission Press who have partnered in the initial printing and distribution of this book.

I'm blessed to be surrounded by great men in my life who are also great fathers: my brother Brad Hamilton and my brothers-in-law Tim Vercellono and Saul Osuna. Thank you for raising amazing kids who have become incredible adults. I love, respect, and honor you.

Most of all, I thank my own family—my wife, Jayme; my son, Justin (and daughter-in-law, Savannah) and my daughter, Jordanne. Together we live this out, often imperfectly but always with the intention of honoring God in our family and loving each other unconditionally. Words aren't enough to express my gratitude to you and for you. I love you…I'm proud of you.

These are the commands, decrees and laws the LORD your God directed me to teach you to observe in the land that you are crossing the Jordan to possess, [2] so that you, your children and their children after them may fear the LORD your God as long as you live by keeping all his decrees and commands that I give you, and so that you may enjoy long life...

[5] Love the LORD your God with all your heart and with all your soul and with all your strength. [6] These commandments that I give you today are to be on your hearts.[7] Impress them on your children. Talk about them when you sit at home and when you walk along the road, when you lie down and when you get up.

DEUTERONOMY 6:1-2,5-7 (NIV)

www.ingramcontent.com/pod-product-compliance
Lightning Source LLC
Chambersburg PA
CBHW081656120626
46550CB00010B/2922